AF485587

VARDHAAN

Twelve Regrets from the Deathbed

A final conversation with my dying grandpa.
Exploring his top regrets and the transformative
power of regret.

Written & published by:

VARDHAAN

Disclaimer:

This book is intended for informational purposes only. The author does not provide any guarantees regarding the results from the use of this information. Always consult a qualified professional for advice specific to your situation.

Chapters of Regrets

I, Him, In the I.C.U

My grandfather's surgery was scheduled for 9:30 AM for his Y-stent insertion, two days after he had a heart attack and was rushed to the hospital.

He had been smoking for fifty years, and I still remember accompanying him along with my grandma when he first sought medical help for his back pain and digestive issues.

The doctor had asked me to wait outside the endoscopy room, and when he appeared out of it, his expression was grave. He invited us into the consultation room.

Looking at my grandpa, the doctor said, "Should I be straightforward about what I found?" My grandpa, knowing what was likely coming, responded, "I'm seventy-nine already. What's the worst that can happen, even if it's death?"

The doctor, after a pause, replied, "It does look like cancer, but you don't have to be worried, there are many modern treatment options available. You look like you're strong enough to handle even the radiation therapy. Let's refer the tumor sample for a biopsy."

I was devastated listening to what doctor told but tried to remain brave for my grandfather, who likely did the same. We all put on a brave front, covering our fear. I offered to take the sample to the laboratory myself and asked my grandfather to head home, and I drove to the clinic to deliver the sample for testing.

As I drove, I reassured myself that he had lived a full life, exceeding the average lifespan. I thought that even if the results were dire, he had no regrets. But I hoped for a slim chance that the tests might come back negative.

At the clinic, I handed over the sample and inquired at the reception about the timeline for the results. "One week," said the receptionist with a tone that felt indifferent to the gravity of the situation.

It wasn't her fault; she was just doing her job. Empathy wasn't part of her role, even though it felt like the report would make a world of difference for us.

When I reached home, everyone was already aware of the situation. My brave grandpa had shared the news with them already, trying to sound upbeat despite the grim prognosis.

A week later, I went to the clinic to pick up the test results. As I walked in, I could sense the weight of potential bad news looming. I paid the fee and took the envelope containing the results. I couldn't wait to get home and so tore open the envelope immediately. My eyes scanned the document quickly until they landed on the word "Negative." I could hardly believe it. The cancer test had come back negative. A wave of relief washed over me.

I drove home as fast as I could, eager to share the news. When I told everyone the test results were negative, there was an outpouring of joy. However, my grandfather's reaction was more complex. He looked at me with a mix of surprise and disbelief. "Let me see that," he said. "I can't believe it's negative." Taking the envelope from my hands.

In that moment, it became clear to me that my grandfather, who had faced the prospect of death with such resignation, might have been ready to let go. The negative result seemed to challenge his expectations and, perhaps, his readiness to move on.

I took the test results to the doctor, eager to show him that his endoscopy had been inaccurate. However, he seemed unfazed when he reviewed the results.

"I expected the results to be positive," he said. "It looked cancerous. Could you bring your grandfather back here? I'd like to take a more thorough sample for another test."

In an instant, all my relief evaporated. Why do doctors always seem to have such pessimistic views? I thought. Still, I agreed to bring my grandfather back and scheduled another visit to the hospital.

The second endoscopy took longer, and I could see my grandfather's frustration as he emerged from the procedure. Who would enjoy having a long tube inserted down their throat? The sample this time seemed more substantial, and a sense of warning settled over me. My fears were confirmed when the results came back positive after another week. The cancer was indeed present. The pessimist doctor was right!

We set about planning the treatment process, consulting numerous doctors and exploring various treatment options. Among them, one doctor's words stood out: "You don't look like one of those patients. You seem strong, and I'm hopeful you'll make a full recovery with treatment."

At that moment, I couldn't help but think how some doctors and hospitals view patients' genuine struggles as mere opportunities for profit and create a false sense of hope.

My poor grandfather, who had nearly lost hope, was buoyed by these optimistic words. It seemed as if the doctor's reassurance sparked a flicker of renewed faith in him. The proposed treatment plan was an intensive combination of surgery, radiation, and chemotherapy. By the time we discovered the cancer, it was already at an advanced stage. Despite this, we clung to hope, believing that perhaps things would work out in the end.

The treatment began swiftly after our consultations. My grandfather underwent a successful surgery, and his mold was prepared for the radiotherapy sessions. While the rest of the family was understandably anxious, my grandfather remained confident as he started his initial rounds of radiotherapy. However, over time, weakness began to take its toll, and his food reflux worsened to the point where he could hardly eat anything.

My grandfather had always been known for his remarkable walking ability; his pace was such that he could easily outpace both youngsters and adults. It was heartbreaking to witness his once brisk walk slow to a shuffle, eventually to the point where he struggled to move at all. After the first round of chemotherapy, his condition deteriorated further. He suffered a minor attack and was rushed to the hospital by ambulance.

After being admitted to the hospital, my grandfather underwent a series of tests and was soon placed in the I.C.U.

The doctors discovered an implication in one of the valves in his throat and determined that a tracheobronchial Y-stent needed to be inserted to enable him to eat and drink again. At that moment, he was weaker than ever, possibly the weakest he had ever been. I could hardly bear to see him in such a fragile state.

His surgery was scheduled for 9:30 AM, two days after his heart attack had been treated. While everyone else was asleep, I decided to visit him in the ICU. With the nurse's permission, I quietly entered the room and saw him resting. As I approached the edge of his bed, he stirred and slowly opened his eyes, offering a gentle smile. He gestured with his hand, making circular motions, inviting me to come around the bed and sit on the stool beside him.

"Looks like this might be the last time I see you," he said quietly. "I may not make it through this." My eyes filled with tears. I tried to reassure him, "It's not that easy to die. It's just a simple Y-stent procedure, and you'll be moved out of the I.C.U as soon as the surgery is completed." He merely nodded, not arguing with me. Perhaps he had a sense of what was to come.

He then pointed to the lever on the bed, indicating he wanted it adjusted. "Do you want to sit up?" I asked. He nodded in agreement. I adjusted the lever, changing the bed's position so it became more like a chair. My grandfather leaned back, wincing in pain as he adjusted to the new position. The numerous tubes and equipment connected to him looked incredibly uncomfortable.

He then said, "I have a few regrets in my life. I've been reflecting all day. Please listen to what I'm about to share and avoid making the same mistakes I did. Will you?"

I said to him, "You've been the best grandfather, father, husband, and a son. What regrets could you possibly have?

There's no such thing as regret in your life. Whatever has happened, has happened for the best."

He smiled faintly and replied, "I'm on my deathbed now, not you. Everything doesn't seem so good when you're about to leave this planet. I understand your perspective and even told myself similarly that whatever happens, happens. I tried to convince myself I had no regrets. But now, I realize that sometimes it's not just about what happens to us, but also about what we might have done differently to influence how things turned out."

"Consider these wise words from an old man and note them down somewhere. Perhaps your grandkids won't have to hear them from you," he said.

I quickly asked the nurse for a pen and paper. She handed me a prescription notepad and a pen, reminding me to leave the I.C.U soon. I told her I would stay for just fifteen more minutes, but she didn't realize that I ended up spending the next few hours talking with my grandfather.

This book details the final conversation I had with my grandfather, his life experiences, and the regrets he felt that every adult and teenager may relate and should act on before it's too late. He wanted to ensure that others don't experience the same level of regret he did on his deathbed. These are his twelve regrets from the deathbed.

I wish I Pursued My Dreams

I always disputed with myself whether I should do what I love or focus on what needs to be done. Often, I ended up doing neither, being too busy to choose one. When I was a kid, my father would tell me that you must work hard, really hard to succeed in life.

"Same with me grandpa! My father says the same thing, I guess all fathers are alike. I never liked this idea 'working hard' it is not exactly inspiring, and if it's hard, why should I do it? I'd rather do something I love." I interrupted.

He responded "Every son is the same too. I used to think just like you and had the same disputes with my father. But you need to realize that every son eventually becomes a father, and when you do, you'll probably say the same things to your kids. This cycle continues. If you want to avoid regrets, understand that there's no substitute for hard work in life. Even when you're doing what you love the most, you'll still need to work hard. 'Hard' doesn't always mean doing something difficult; it can also mean repeating something over and over again, doing it when you don't feel like doing it because it needs to be done."

Tiny droplets of water were falling onto a rock continuously next to a river. When it first droplet landed, the rock felt a gentle pleasure rather than pain. This continued day after day, with the droplets never ceasing. After a few years, the rock noticed a dent forming, and eventually, a perforation. The droplets now pass through the rock and make it other side.

This illustrates how even small actions, when repeated over time, can lead to significant results. You might enjoy performing these small actions, but the repeated effort is what constitutes hard work. And that's the key to success.

I wish I had pursued my dreams at every stage of my life. When I was in my high school, there were always film shoots happening on the outskirts of the city. The area where I lived was dotted with ancient monumental constructions that served as backdrops for historical movies.

My friends and I would often skip class to watch the shoots. I was mesmerized by the actors. The way they dressed, the cars they drove, the food they ate on set, and the admiration they received from fans. I longed to live a life like that.

One day, my friends and I hurried to a shooting location because our favorite actor was filming there. When we finally saw him, we were starstruck. His presence was captivating, his long hair flowing, his vibrant costume, and his majestic personality. People around him looked at him as if he were from another world.

I stood there, mouth open in awe, and slowly said, "Damn! I wish I could become an actor like him someday." My thoughts were louder than I realized, and my friends burst into laughter. "You? An actor?" they said. "You can't even shake his hand. We're only meant to watch them from afar and enjoy their movies. We'll never become actors ourselves."

Their reaction left me feeling anguished. Although it shook my confidence and nearly buried my newly-born dream, I took a deep breath and said, "I can be whatever I want to be.

What's wrong with wanting to become an actor? He must have had similar thoughts when he first dreamed of becoming an actor."

"And shaking his hand isn't a big deal," I said confidently.

"He wouldn't mind shaking hands with a fan. I'm going to shake his hand before he leaves here," I declared. Whenever there were shoots, entry points were blocked and a guard was stationed at the gate. I took my challenge seriously and was determined to shake my favorite actor's hand no matter what.

I asked my friends to keep an eye on me and ran toward the gate. The guard, hired from the local town, turned out to be someone I knew. He was my brother's friend's uncle. I hurried over to him, reminding him of a past encounter and weaving a few stories we had shared, playfully accusing him of having forgotten them.

"Did you get to meet the actor?" I asked.

"We can't meet them. I'm here to do my job, and I won't be allowed inside. Once I'm paid, I'm done," he replied.

"Don't you feel bad about not meeting him?" I asked.

"I do, he's an amazing actor. But there's nothing I can do about it," he said.

"Take me inside. We both can go and meet him," I suggested.

"I can't do that. If someone sees me letting you in, they'll kick me out and I won't get paid for the work I've done so far," he explained.

"Nobody will see us, Uncle. It's their lunch break. This actor steps away during his break and won't be with the crew. He won't mind us; we can shake his hand and be back before he rejoins the rest of the crew," I persuaded him.

We snuck inside together, carefully avoiding the crew members and equipment. We spotted the actor resting under a tree, away from the crowd, with only one of his personal guards standing nearby, looking in the other direction. I asked the uncle to keep an eye out for me so I could approach the actor first. Considering I was just a student, I hoped he wouldn't be too upset if I managed to meet him briefly.

I ran up to the actor and exclaimed, "Sir! I watch all your movies and am so excited to see you. My friends said I could never shake your hand, so I challenged them to prove them wrong. I also dream of becoming an actor like you someday." I spoke quickly, not giving him a chance to react.

He looked at me with a gentle smile and asked, "How did you get in here?"

I said, "I sneaked in quietly. Sir, can I shake your hand?" My excitement was so intense that my teeth were showing uncontrollably.

He smiled and replied, "Of course! So, you want to be an actor?" as he shook my hand.

I said, "Yes, sir."

In that case, he said, "You'll need to learn acting and perform a dialogue for me. I'll be back here in six months for my next movie shoot. Come and meet me then, and I'll have a role for you in my film."

I was stunned. "Absolutely! I'll do that," I exclaimed, jumping in the air with joy.

The security guard nearby noticed me and approached in anger. The actor signaled to him to calm down and asked him to let me through the gate.

"Sir! I'll definitely see you again," I said as I quickly made my way out.

That day, my dream of becoming an actor grew stronger. I wasn't sure if the actor genuinely intended to give me an opportunity or if he was just trying to avoid disappointing me. Regardless, I was determined to practice acting. I saved up money to buy books with monologues from his movies.

I remember practicing the dialogues and trying to master a few expressions. I quickly realized it wasn't as easy as I'd thought. I struggled with remembering the lines and began to question if acting was really for me. I found excuses, telling myself I was too busy studying, that I was too young and had plenty of time to pursue this dream.

I kept forgetting the lines, and they seemed too tough to remember. Doubts crept in, and I began to think I couldn't act. I even told myself that the actor was probably joking and that no way would he offer a role to some random person like me.

I let my dream die. When the actor returned six months later, I didn't even bother going to the movie shooting spot.

My aspiration to become an actor had faded deep into the recesses of my mind.

Months later, I ran into the uncle who had helped me get inside the shooting spot. Whenever I saw him, I tried to avoid him, fearing he might punish me for risking his job. But one day, he caught me off guard.

"I'm sorry, Uncle. I didn't want to jeopardize your job, I wanted to meet the actor that day," I confessed.

He replied, "I'm not sure where you were, but the actor did notice me with you. When he returned for the shoot, I was stationed at the gate again. He sent his staff to ask about you. I couldn't recall who you were. Later, I found out the actor was looking for you to audition for a role in his upcoming movie. They ended up hiring another kid from a different place."

I couldn't believe what I heard. My dream of becoming an actor was real, but I had been too lazy and arrogant to pursue it. Instead, I had made excuses because it was hard. Now, I deeply regret not seizing that opportunity.

Of course, it was supposed to be hard. If it were easy, everyone would have it, and you wouldn't value it as much. The difficulty is what makes it valuable.

"You could've been a great actor by now, Grandpa, if you had pursued your dream that day. It's sad, but I understand your feelings now." I said.

Not just that, there were many phases of my life where I didn't pursue my dreams, whether they were big or small. It's not about the size of the dreams, but the thought that inspires them. Dreams have meaning; they carry a message for you. The journey itself will teach you something valuable.

The pain of giving up is heavier than the effort of staying on track and persisting until you succeed.

Don't fear judgment when you share your dreams with others. If you're afraid of their judgment, it's better not to share your dreams with them. Before letting someone judge your dreams, you should also evaluate them yourself. Ask if they are truly achievable or if you're simply dreaming of the impossible. Remember, dreaming big is different from dreaming of what's unattainable.

Dreams are often distant from reality. When I say that, I don't mean they can't become real, but rather that they take time to materialize. It's like seeing an oasis in a hot desert. At first glance, it seems like a mirage, something that doesn't exist. You might run towards it only to find nothing. However, if you persist and travel further to the town with a water supply, you will definitely find water. Similarly, while your dreams may seem elusive at first, perseverance will eventually lead you to achieve them.

In the desert, when you're thirsty, it's better to seek out a real town nearby rather than chasing after illusory ponds that don't exist. When you're striving to achieve something, focus on goals that are tangible and attainable. Don't be misled by dreams that are purely imaginary, unattainable, or just empty words.

I'm not suggesting you should dream small. I encourage you to dream big and ambitiously. Even if your dreams involve things that have never been accomplished or seen before, ensure that your hope and confidence are grounded in reality. Aim for a viable outcome rather than just ending up with a mere imaginary prototype.

True failure isn't defined by not reaching your goal but by giving up halfway through the journey. But how can you know if you're on the right path, if the path has a real destination, or even where you are on that path? It's a mix of many factors: your dream, your efforts, a bit of luck, perseverance, and the wisdom to understand and adapt to your dream.

Thomas Edison tried thousands of times to invent the light bulb, while someone with a fantastical dream of flying like Superman, dressed in a costume, ended up breaking bones after just ten attempts.

When you dream, you're essentially trying to create something out of nothing and make it a reality. The very concept of pursuing a dream can sometimes seem overly romanticized or unrealistic. It's unfair to expect dreams to materialize quickly.

Dreams often carry significant meaning. I'm not talking about the dreams you have while you're asleep, but the aspirations and visions that occupy your mind when you're awake. These conscious dreams, about becoming someone, achieving something, or reaching somewhere are important indicators of what might be possible for you. If you can envision it, there's a reason behind that vision.

Sometimes, the dreams you pursue may not come from your own imagination but from someone who recognizes your potential and interests. There's nothing wrong with chasing such dreams, but it's important to assess their feasibility. Every dream might seem impossible at first, but that doesn't mean you should dismiss it outright. Analyzing a dream involves evaluating the skills, time, resources, and passion required to achieve it.

For example:

- Dreaming of flying on an airplane is achievable if you work hard enough to purchase a ticket.

- Dreaming of becoming a pilot requires a greater commitment: you'll need to work diligently, show perseverance, practice regularly, and invest in learning the necessary skills, including taking flying lessons and seeking mentorship.

- Dreaming of para-gliding between mountains involves even more effort: you need to start with basic para-gliding, conquer your fear of heights, endure potential failures, and remain dedicated and passionate to achieve the goal safely.

- Dreaming of inventing a new airplane that uses a quarter of the fuel compared to existing models is an ambitious goal, but with rigorous experimentation, deep study, and countless hours of hard work and persistence, it could be within reach.

Conversely, dreaming of stopping a flying airplane with your hands while in space, like a Superhero, is an unrealistic fantasy rather than a feasible goal. Pursuing such an unattainable dream could end up being a waste of time and energy.

Dreams are valuable and worth pursuing if they are achievable with dedication and effort. The key is to differentiate between what is realistically possible and what is purely imaginary.

Sometimes, your dreams are influenced or fueled by others. They may not always be out of jealousy or competition, but sometimes because people encourage you to improve, strive for better, and pursue greater goals. Being irresponsible towards those dreams is not a sign of strength but of weakness. Smart decisions involve avoiding situations that could lead to trouble. Irresponsible actions are the pitfalls in life, and claiming to be smart by avoiding responsibilities whether for yourself or others is a sign of weakness rather than strength.

I often regret not pursuing the dreams set for me by others.

When I was in my early thirties, juggling a busy work life with a family, your grandmother and our kids, it felt like every day was a battle. Your grandmother suggested that I invest money and partner with her brother in a business venture. Her hope was that this would increase our profits and income, enabling us to buy a house for our family.

She suggested this because she saw a potential path for me and set that vision. Often, when someone tells us what to do, even if it's someone we love, we might react defensively or with disinterest. It's not always because we don't understand their advice but because it diverges from what we initially envisioned. I reacted the same way. I told her it was impossible for me to find additional time for a business or explore other income opportunities given my workload at the office. I reassured her that being in my early thirties meant we still had time to buy a house.

My wife brought it up a few times and explained why she believed I could pursue this dream. She recognized the potential and skills I had that could be valuable in partnering with her brother's business. She was confident that if I genuinely tried other investment options, I could generate a profit and improve our family's financial situation.

She also emphasized how working hard at an early age would lead to a happier life later on. She reassured me that it was okay to feel tired or to think that managing the business might take additional time. She pointed out that I was capable of handling it now, and that as I grew older, it would become more challenging to pursue such opportunities. She explained how having savings and owning a house would benefit our children, providing them with better lives.

But I barely paid attention. I adhered to my own philosophy of not rushing things and dealing with them in their own time. I believed in this approach and chose not to pursue the dreams my wife suggested.

After few months, one of my friends in the after-work group gradually started to drift away from our social gatherings and late-night discussions. We used to spend time debating politics, economic trends, country wars, and office gossip, topics that didn't contribute to our financial growth. That's when I realized that engaging in conversations merely to win an argument or to demonstrate that you have something to say yields no real results. Effective conversations should be either financially beneficial or intellectually enriching.

While it's important to have lighthearted banter and enjoy nonsensical discussions with friends and family,

there comes a point when you need to stop and prioritize more meaningful aspects of life.

When my friend disappeared from the group, we eventually stopped noticing his absence. A few months later, I ran into him and mentioned how we missed him at our gathering.

He replied that he had been busy working on building his new house. I was surprised and asked him how he managed to fund it.

He explained that he had been working on multiple investment opportunities, including collaborating with a financial consultant. He also mentioned investing a portion of his investment profits into his father-in-law's goods export business.

I was curious how he managed this, given how demanding and exhausting office work was. He replied that he had focused on eliminating unimportant tasks from his daily routine, prioritizing investment and money-making activities while avoiding activities that didn't benefit him. This was why he hadn't been attending our late-night gathering.

I asked him about the importance of having fun and enjoying life. "Why burden yourself with so much work? You only live once," I said.

He replied, "I know, and that's why I work hard. Once the time passes by, it becomes harder to chase this dream. I don't want to be weak and vulnerable. I need to provide for my family and buy them whatever they need. My wife supports me in this, and she's the one pushing me to pursue this dream. I'd regret it if I didn't go after it."

At that moment, I still didn't fully grasp his perspective. It was later that I realized how, as people age, they often become too stubborn to admit their mistakes. They find excuses and convince themselves they are incapable or irresponsible, using these justifications to defend themselves against the world. Regardless of the reasons, this attitude ultimately leads to failure.

But after hearing him. I told myself a profound lesson: "It doesn't matter if I'm wealthy or earn more money. People often chase after more, missing out on the simple joys of life. I don't want to be part of that race. I'll teach my children that it's not about having a bigger house but about having a happy home that truly matters."

But those were just excuses. I was too prideful to admit my shortcomings. Sure, my children could be happy in a smaller house, but they'd likely be even happier in a bigger one. The issue isn't that a larger house is the key to happiness, but who wouldn't want a better living situation if given the chance? While people often say they don't need more, but no one turns down an opportunity for a better life if it's offered for free. It's easy to claim that it doesn't matter when we can't achieve it, but deep down, we all desire improvement and want more.

That's how I came to regret not pursuing that dream, my wife's dream, and mine as well.

There are different kinds of dreams you experience, whether awake or asleep. Now, you must learn to distinguish which dreams are worth pursuing and which ones should be questioned or set aside.

Type of Dream	Name	Description
Dreams that defy reality	Fantastical Dreams	Dreams featuring scenarios that are impossible or highly improbable, such as flying on an elephant.
Dreams with personal significance	Reflective Dreams	Dreams that draw meaning from your current life situations or emotions, mirroring your thoughts and concerns.
Dreams about future ambitions	Aspirational Dreams	Dreams centered on achieving long-term goals or desires, like owning a Ferrari.

Dreams lacking logical structure	Absurd Dreams	Dreams characterized by illogical or nonsensical elements, often without clear meaning or relevance.

Fantastical dreams: These dreams are those of pure imagination. You might experience them while you're asleep or even when you're wide awake, whether you're idle, alone, surrounded by familiar faces, or deeply immersed in tasks. These dreams often involve scenarios that are highly improbable or impossible in reality. For example, you'll never fly while sitting on an elephant or you'll step into a magical paradise randomly opening the door of your backyard.

These dreams are not worth pursuing. Chasing such fantasies is akin to pursuing something that doesn't exist. Trying to recall and live within these dreams is merely a waste of time too. While they might provide temporary pleasure, you can't consistently chase after emotions tied to fiction. The more you focus on these fantasies, the further you stray from engaging with and appreciating reality.

Unless you aspire to become a great storyteller or writer, there's no need to memorize these fantastical dreams. Your mind can generate countless such scenarios beating any kind of artificial intelligence with your natural intelligence.

Reflective dreams: Reflective dreams are those that arise from your current situations, emotions, thoughts, and concerns, often occurring while you're asleep. Should you pursue them? No. They are merely reflections of what you're feeling at that moment and don't necessarily signify anything significant. Worrying too much about them can trap you in an endless loop of anxiety.

While reflective dreams themselves don't carry deeper meaning, they can serve as reminders of your current state of thoughts, conditions and emotions. Where you are, what you're doing, and what needs attention. For instance, a student who is anxious about exams might dream of failing, skipping the exam, or forgetting their answers. When they wake up, such dreams can feel overwhelming. However, these dreams are simply reflections of their fear and anxiety about the exams.

They don't imply that these scenarios will come true. Instead, the human brain tends to create various scenarios based on the emotions it's experiencing. If the student dwells on these dreams and allows them to dictate their reality, the fears could indeed become self-fulfilling. The best approach is to use these dreams as a prompt to take practical steps, such as studying diligently and addressing their exam-related fears.

Sometimes, these dreams can be challenging to interpret and may not offer clear insights. When that's the case, it's best not to overanalyze them or try to derive meaning from them or google "What does this dream mean?", I know your generation likes googling everything but hear me out, they mean nothing.

Instead, recognize them as reflections of your current emotional state and don't let them instill unnecessary fear. Often, they are simply exaggerated manifestations of your existing worries, as the human brain tends to amplify feelings and create elaborate scenarios around them.

Aspirational Dreams: These are dreams about your desires, goals, and aspirations. They often occur when you're awake, fully conscious, and engaged with your senses. Unlike reflective dreams, which are reactions to your current emotional state, aspirational dreams should be taken seriously. The origin of these dreams, why you have them may not be as important as evaluating their feasibility.

Often, these dreams are influenced by external factors, but it's crucial to assess whether they are genuinely achievable and aligned with your true will. Even if the source of the aspiration is unclear or forgotten, the dream itself holds significance. For instance, you might have a strong desire to visit Switzerland, but you may not remember exactly where that desire originated, perhaps from a picture, a video, or a person's recommendation.

What matters is how you approach this aspiration. If you genuinely want to pursue this dream, you should focus on making it a reality. Evaluate the feasibility, set clear goals, and take actionable steps toward achieving it. Even if the initial source of your aspiration is forgotten, the dream itself can provide motivation and direction.

In summary, while the origin of aspirational dreams might be less significant, their pursuit can be highly meaningful. Ensure that these dreams are grounded in reality, validate their feasibility, and commit to making them happen.

So, these are the dreams that must be taken seriously and pursued.

These are dreams about your desires, goals, and aspirations. They should be approached with intention and action. Dreaming something whether big or small requires more than just wishing for it; it involves a concrete plan of action.

When you dream about something, whether it's as simple as buying an ice cream or as ambitious as starting a business, you must approach it with a structured plan if you aim to achieve it efficiently. For example, even a small dream like buying an ice cream involves a series of actions: planning when to go, choosing the mode of transport, selecting the ice cream shop, deciding on the flavor, and managing the budget. Each step requires thought and effort. If you take steps without proper actions, you might taste a bland ice cream or never find one when you want it.

Planning: To turn a dream into reality, you need to follow a series of planned actions. Writing down your aspirations is a crucial first step. After you've written them down, transform them into a plan or project. Break down the steps required to achieve your dream, set milestones, and create a timeline.

Action Steps: For any dream, big or small, achieving it efficiently involves taking deliberate actions. Start by outlining your goals, identifying the resources you'll need, and setting specific, actionable tasks. This methodical approach will help you navigate from the dream stage to tangible results.

In essence, pursuing your dreams involves more than just having them; it requires a clear, actionable plan and the dedication to follow through. Whether your dream is to enjoy a small pleasure or achieve a significant milestone, structured planning and consistent effort are key to making it a reality.

Break down your big project into yearly, monthly, and daily tasks. This approach is crucial because we often focus on the final result rather than the steps required to get there. When you envision a large dream and write it down, the sheer scale can feel overwhelming and make you doubt your ability to achieve it. By concentrating on smaller, manageable actions, you avoid becoming discouraged by the overall scope.

A big dream can seem unattainable if you focus solely on the final outcome from the start. Instead, break it into smaller milestones and focus on the next step rather than the end goal.

This approach helps you stay motivated and makes the journey to achieving your dream more manageable.

If you embark on a journey of a thousand miles in your car, the sheer distance can be overwhelming. At the very start, you might feel restless and doubt your ability to cover the entire journey. The thought of traveling a thousand miles might even make you consider giving up before you've driven a single mile.

Instead, approach your journey with a structured action plan. Break the thousand-mile trip into manageable segments. For example, divide the journey into three or four days, with checkpoints at intervals like one hundred, two hundred, and five hundred miles. By focusing on reaching each checkpoint rather than the entire distance, the journey becomes more manageable and less daunting. This way, you maintain motivation and make steady progress toward your goal.

So, when you start your car, shift your focus from the daunting thousand-mile end goal to the first checkpoint at a hundred miles. After you get to first checkpoint, reward yourself with a nap, a tasty meal and then start your journey. This way, your journey becomes about reaching that initial milestone where you can rest, relax, and rejuvenate before moving on to the next segment.

By concentrating on reaching each hundred-mile checkpoint, the journey feels more manageable and achievable. It transforms a seemingly impossible task into a series of doable steps. I often gave up on big dreams because I focused solely on the end result. Without immediate milestones, the journey felt overwhelming, and I lost motivation. By breaking down the journey into smaller, more attainable checkpoints, you make progress feel more achievable and keep your momentum going.

Perseverance, patience, and a solid plan are crucial for achieving your dreams. Remember, dreams are not just what you see while sleeping; they are the ones that keep you awake, driving you to strive and succeed.

And finally, there are absurd dreams, these dreams are illogical and irrelevant, born from your brain's imaginative storytelling. You might dream of talking pineapples, a tiger with a trunk, or growing diamonds on trees. These dreams make no sense and are best ignored. Discussing their absurdity is a waste of your valuable time. They are more about brain maintenance work than actionable goals. Just let your mind create these notions; don't let them distract you from pursuing what truly matters.

I wish I was more Courageous

Remember, kid, courage isn't about not feeling fear, it's about overcoming it. When you're forced to be courageous, it means pushing yourself to confront your fears. Many people, including myself, used to think that brave people don't experience fear, but that's not the case. They know what fear is; they just overcome it.

Fear is a feeling, just like hunger, anger, sorrow, joy, or even sensations like sleepiness, tiredness, and boredom. Not feeling something isn't something to be proud of; having emotions is a sign of a healthy, functioning mind and body. Imagine if you stopped feeling hungry or lost the ability to feel happy for the rest of your life. Would you want that kind of existence? If such a thing happened, you'd likely seek medical help immediately to understand what's wrong. Why? Because feeling is a crucial part of what makes us human.

Because when you lack a feeling, it's a sign that something might need fixing. So why avoid fear? If you don't experience fear, you should see a repairman of your body, a doctor. Embrace fear, but learn to overcome it. Let it spark within you, so you can put it out before it consumes you.

"But I always saw you as a brave man, Grandpa! When were you not courageous?" I asked.

"I learned to overcome fear by the time you saw me as brave," he replied. "I have a few regrets about not being courageous when you didn't yet see it in me."

"What are those regrets?" I asked, curiosity piqued.

He smiled and continued, "What do you do when you're afraid?".

I thought for a moment and replied, "It depends. Sometimes I try to overcome it, and other times I just make it worse by overthinking."

He nodded thoughtfully. "That's exactly what I went through. I learned that fear doesn't disappear; it's about how you handle it. My regrets are the times I let fear paralyze me instead of facing it head-on. It's a process of learning and growing, and it's never too late to get better at it."

Fair enough. Let's delve into what fear really is.

Fear often revolves around the idea of things turning out differently than you want them to or the potential loss of someone or something valuable, and something bad happening to you or your loved ones. You might fear the dark because you imagine there's someone lurking in it who could harm you. Or you might be anxious about a fight, worried that someone might break your nose. You could also fear losing someone dear to you. These are different fears, but they all share a common thread: the possibility of something happening that you don't want.

You're never afraid of things going the way you hope they will. Fear is always tied to the potential of unwanted outcomes.

Sometimes, you need to accept that it's okay for things to go wrong because it exposes you to the truth or what's right. Often, what you want may not be what you truly need, and events might need to unfold against your wishes to reveal their true purpose.

Fear can cloud your perception and prevent you from facing reality, while courage enables you to confront it. For example, if you fear the dark, your imagination may conjure up countless threats. Only through courage will you discover that there's nothing to fear in the darkness.

I regret not being courageous at times in my life. If I had faced those moments with bravery, the outcomes might have been different. Fear is abstract and can manifest in various ways, often complicating outcomes. Fear itself isn't inherently bad. Sometimes, you don't need to completely conquer your fear; you just need to manage it.

For instance, if you're afraid of heights, you might gradually ease that fear by reassuring yourself that you're safe. But it's important not to overcome your fear to the point where you disregard it entirely. If you lose all sense of caution and act recklessly, like jumping off a building with the confidence of Batman, you risk serious consequences.

Balance is key. Manage your fear, don't let it paralyze you, but also don't let it disappear entirely and lead you into danger.

Imagine a see-saw: when you sit on one end, you need some amount of weight on the other end to balance and lift yourself up. On one side, there's fear; on the other, courage. When you're afraid, courage needs to counterbalance that fear to help you rise and see the reality behind it. Reality is like a beautiful scenery that can only be seen from the top of the see-saw.

However, if there's no courage, you'll remain stuck and unable to see that reality. Conversely, if courage outweighs fear excessively, you risk being propelled too quickly and harshly, like being thrown into the sky and crashing down, which can lead to serious consequences.

For instance, when I was in university, a buddy of mine boldly challenged a student from another class who was taller and stronger. He took on the challenge with such fearless courage that it far outweighed his fear without letting him assess his capabilities. His overabundance of courage led him to leap into a dangerous situation without considering the risks, resulting in him breaking his teeth.

So, it's important to balance your courage and fear carefully. You need enough courage to overcome fear and see the truth but not so much that you disregard fear's warnings and put yourself in harm's way. But imagine if you don't put enough weight on the courage side at all you'll remain stuck on the ground, missing out on opportunities and unable to rise above your fears.

Courage isn't solely about taking risks. It also involves doing the right things, standing up for what's right, and choosing the right times to act.

True courage is about finding that balance: enough courage to rise above your fears and seize opportunities, but not so much that you leap recklessly into danger.

Whether it's a minor situation or a major one, it's crucial to voice out courageously. I remember a time when I was standing in line to buy a ticket for a local act starring a famous singer. Back then, before the days of the internet and online booking, everything was done offline, and you had to stand in queues if there were many people.

When I arrived at the performance theater, I was excited to see the long line, as it meant the show was popular. I waited patiently as the queue slowly shortened, and only a few people were left in front of me. Just as I was looking forward to my turn, a group of four strong, imposing individuals entered and bypassed the queue. They looked like they could be intimidating if confronted, so I didn't say anything.

I watched an elderly man behind me and, feeling sympathetic for his long wait, I allowed him to go ahead of me. However, when it was finally my turn, I was disheartened to find that the elderly man, whom I had let pass, had bought the last ticket. I was left feeling disappointed and angry with myself for not speaking up.

I regretted not standing up and saying, "Hey, I've been waiting in line just like everyone else. You can't cut in like this. Please go to the back of the queue." I let fear control me, even though I knew that the pain of feeling like a coward was worse than facing a confrontation. While it's not always wise to engage in conflicts in public spaces, there are times when it's essential to assert yourself.

Had I voiced my concern courageously that day, others in the line might have supported me, and I would have felt braver. Although it was "just" a ticket, the regret of not taking action still lingers. It reminds me that being courageous means standing up for yourself, even in seemingly small situations.

"Come on, Grandpa! It happens to almost everyone. There's nothing to regret about it. Sometimes it's better to just let it go and not argue with fools and say 'yes'," I said.

"Yes," he replied.

Understanding his wittiness, I said "It doesn't matter actually if you're not brave in such small situations yielding no impact, I believe bravery is most needed when you're in the toughest and grand situations where your bravery is extremely rewarding."

He took a while and responded, let me tell you a small story:

A group of five fishermen went out to fishing every day. Among them, one fisherman never caught any fish. While the other four worked hard by preparing their nets, sharpening their tools, preparing bait, and rowing their boats out to the middle of the ocean the fifth fisherman would simply take a nap and then return home.

When the other fishermen asked him about his lack of effort, he would reply, "I'm not interested in catching the small fish that are in this ocean. I know that someday a huge fish will pass by us, and only I will catch it. This fish will be so large that it will provide food for the entire town. Until then, please share some of your small fish with me for my meals."

The fishermen agreed to share their catch with the fifth man, and this arrangement continued for a while. The four fishermen caught small fish while the fifth one took his nap and enjoyed the fruits of their labor.

One day, the four fishermen had had enough. They asked the fifth one, "We're extremely tired of your behavior and we're wondering if we'll ever see you catch that big fish you keep talking about."

To which he replied, "I will, I will. Just let me find a big fish."

The four fishermen were furious and told him they would take him to a place where he could catch a big fish and asked him to do so. To this, he responded, "What's the hurry?"

Ignoring his words, the four fishermen rowed their boats to the middle of the ocean, where they believed they could find larger and more dangerous fish. When they reached the spot, they handed the fishing equipment to the fifth fisherman and asked him to throw the net first.

The fifth fisherman, timidly, cast the net, but it didn't open properly and simply sank straight into the ocean. The other fishermen looked at him and asked, "Do you even know how to fish?"

The fifth fisherman then revealed, "I'm not actually a fisherman at all. I don't have any job. I only pretended to be a fisherman so I could share in the fish caught by the rest of you."

Realizing they had been deceived, the four fishermen treated the fifth man as if he were the big fish he had always talked about. They captured him in the net and brought him back with them.

Similarly, I can't promise to accomplish bigger goals if I'm not handling the smaller goals. If I'm not putting efforts with smaller actions, I'll never be able to put larger actions. If I can't walk, I'll never learn to sprint. Smaller actions lead to bigger actions which in turn lead to bigger results.

So, If I'm not courageous in minor situations, I can't expect to be brave in more significant ones, the more dangerous ones.

The more I act fearlessly in smaller, inconvenient situations, I'll learn to act with more courage in bigger situations.

Courage isn't just a reaction to individual situations; it's a mindset shaped by consistent patterns of behavior. So is the fear.

It's not about being courageous in every single moment, but about developing a habitual way of responding bravely over time.

Though I promised myself I would be more courageous, I didn't take action. The next time someone took my place, when someone said something hurtful, or when I saw someone doing something wrong, I remained silent. I couldn't assemble the courage to act.

There was a time at my office when a new manager replaced a kind and considerate one. This new manager was strict and had poor communication skills. When things didn't go as he expected, he would not only be blunt but also make false allegations and cross personal boundaries to insult others.

One day, I missed a deadline for submitting my work, and he started yelling at me without listening to my explanation. I was furious but lacked the courage to tell him to stop and not cross those boundaries. I left the office feeling disappointed and frustrated.

The next day, I noticed he was unusually quiet and not engaging with anyone. Curious, I asked a colleague what had happened. He explained that after I left the previous day, the manager had treated another worker in the same aggressive manner. This worker had stood up to him, yelled back, and made it clear that such behavior was unacceptable. The manager, embarrassed and afraid of losing his job if everyone reacted this way, had been quiet ever since.

I found myself in a similar situation but failed to voice out and act courageously. It's crucial to speak up for yourself when necessary. When someone crosses boundaries, tries to insult, disrespect, or harm you, it's important to have the courage to stand up for yourself.

You have to prioritize yourself and not let yourself down by taking courageous actions. It's essential to be wise about when to confront a situation and when to remain silent. You might not be able to take on ten people physically, but you can certainly address one person with courage and assertiveness through your words. Balancing bravery with judgement is key to standing up for yourself effectively.

Likewise, in a classroom, students should have the courage to speak up for themselves or the class, and if they have an opinion or a question, they should voice it. Similarly, in a meeting, if an employee has a brilliant idea that could benefit the company or a question because they don't understand something, they should ask it.

After all, what's the worst that can happen if your question is deemed "stupid"? The response could be an answer, a suggestion to find out on your own, or simply an acknowledgment that there isn't an answer to such question. That's perfectly fine.

People are generally too busy with their own lives, responsibilities, and problems to dwell on your mistakes or even to discuss your contributions for long. They have their own concerns and make mistakes themselves. If everyone makes errors, why should you let the fear of judgment hold you back?

As a student, you probably had many questions during lectures and hesitated to ask them. You might have worried that others would think your questions were silly or wondered how you didn't know the answer to something that seemed basic. Correct?

"Yes, Grandpa!" Many a times. I had so many questions but hesitated to ask them. Every time I had a question, I'd wait to see if the professor would bring it up himself. Sometimes, professors would even ask, "Did nobody have this question?" and I'd regret not asking it.

What's worse, there were times when I had questions that I was afraid to ask because of embarrassment or overthinking. Then, someone else would ask the same question and be praised for it. I used to blame myself all the way home on those days.

My Grandpa replied, absolutely! Most of us have been there. Every time you let fear hold you back, someone else who isn't afraid seizes the opportunity while you miss out.

But I appreciate that you sometimes waited, hoping the professor would address your questions even if you didn't ask them. That shows patience and a willingness to listen, even in the face of fear. It's not about continuing to fear, but about finding a balance, being patient and letting things unfold while also building the courage to speak up when needed.

Winston Churchill once said, "Courage is what it takes to stand up and speak; courage is also what it takes to sit down and listen."

Sometimes, people become so courageous that they create an imbalance between fear and courage. They may voice their opinions so forcefully that they fail to be receptive to others' feedback and constantly deny the validity of different perspectives. This isn't courage; it's arrogance or ignorance.

Remember, kid, having a strong personality and firmly believing in your principles are important, but it's equally vital to recognize that your perception is shaped by your own understanding, experiences, situations, and feelings. True courage involves not just speaking up but also listening and being open to different viewpoints.

Perspectives can differ depending on people, time, and place. As these factors change, so too will your perspectives, if not all of them, at least some. Change is inevitable and essential for growth.

Don't be arrogant in holding just one way of looking at things and get offended when someone disagrees. When you're overly courageous in arguing and asserting your opinions solely to dismiss someone else's, you're merely feeding your ego and wasting time and energy that could be better spent.

True growth comes from being open to change and valuing diverse viewpoints.

Courage also involves accepting your mistakes and faults. It takes real bravery to admit you're wrong and to say you're sorry.

When you lack the courage to acknowledge your errors, you might resort to making excuses or displaying arrogance. True courage lies in owning up to your mistakes and showing humility.

Many times, in my life, I used all my energy and time to prove my point, even when I was clearly wrong, whether at work, at home, or with friends. Whenever I realized my mistakes, I would dodge them and refuse to let others point out my faults. That's not courage!

Courage also means acknowledging when you're wrong. It's about trying again, despite failures and rejections. You mustn't give up at the first sign of defeat. True courage is standing up every time you fall. It's not about never falling, but about having the strength to get up repeatedly.

When you go for a job interview and face rejection, or attend another interview only to be rejected again, don't let fear stop you from trying again. It takes courage to face rejection and keep going.

If you start your first business and it fails, take the time to review your errors, learn from them, and try again. If you fail a second time, repeat the process. Every failure is a lesson. Don't let the fear of failing again hold you back. Be courageous enough to stand up, learn from your mistakes, take corrective actions, and keep moving forward.

Let me tell you a story about courage, in a distant town, it was believed that diamonds lay hidden beneath the surface. The local legend said that ancient kings from neighboring kingdoms had used the town as a treasure repository storing diamonds and gold there during the historical times. It was also thought that the town was a natural diamond producer.

Whenever it rained in that town, at least one or two people would find a diamond each rainy season. A poor man from a neighboring town, who had lost his home and means of sustenance due to a thunderstorm and heavy downpour, decided to seek his fortune in the diamond-rich town. With no job to support his family or repair his house, he believed in the possibility of getting lucky and set out on his quest.

Every day, he would rise early and meticulously search every part of the town, hoping to find his lucky stones.

He divided the town into fourteen sections and planned to search each part in a phased approach. The town was small and remote, and when it rained, it rained uniformly across the entire area.

His search had to be thorough, covering every corner to find the diamonds, as luck alone might not be enough. He knew he needed to be thorough in his efforts to ensure he didn't miss any potential finds.

He had planned his search to span four months and began as soon as the rainy season arrived. Dividing the town into fourteen sections, he meticulously searched each area, often digging the open spaces with a long stick and tools he carried.

Weeks went by, and despite his efforts, he found no diamonds. His hope began to wane, and he grew increasingly anxious about the situation at home. With all his hopes pinned on finding diamonds, his fears started to overshadow his determination. Each day he woke up dreading the possibility of returning home empty-handed. With every failed attempt, his fear intensified, the fear of losing, the fear of having to try again.

Throughout his search, he would often hear neighborhood gossip about others finding diamonds, which only deepened his sadness and frustration. He began to blame his luck and his efforts for his lack of success.

The four months eventually passed, and he had found nothing but dust and worthless rocks. He had completed thirteen sections of the town, leaving only one part to search. His fear reached its peak as he realized that after investing four months of his time, if he failed in this last section, he would end up with nothing. The thought of starting over from scratch filled him with dread and despair.

The night before he was set to search the final part of the town, he couldn't sleep. The rainy season had made the town cozy and cold, but he was drenched in sweat from fear and despair. He constantly battled with thoughts of giving up, convincing himself that he wouldn't be able to face the possibility of completing the search without finding a single diamond. He considered abandoning his quest, deciding to return home so he wouldn't have to entirely blame himself for searching the entire town without success.

As tears of fear and sadness welled up in his eyes, he remembered the words of his late father: "Do it when you are afraid, do it when you have lost everything, do it even if you feel you won't win. Do it with courage, do it with conviction, do it right. When you fear something before it happens, you've feared it more than necessary. Take the chance and give your best. The best is not about full force but the right force."

After recalling his father's words, he found a new sense of courage. He took some time to reflect on his search, analyzing the mistakes he had made along the way and noting down corrective actions he could take. Despite his persistent belief that he was simply unlucky, he resolved to face the final part of the search with renewed determination.

He decided that he would not let fear of failure paralyze him any longer. Even if he didn't find any diamonds, he would leave with the satisfaction of having worked hard and given his best. With this mindset, he approached the final section with a sense of purpose and resolve, ready to search thoroughly and correctly, no matter the outcome.

He woke up the next day and continued his search, but by the end of the day, he had found nothing. His fear resurfaced, but he managed to overcome it. The same happened on the second, third, fourth, and fifth days.

On the sixth day, just three days before his search was set to conclude, he ventured into a barren farmland adjacent to a large pond. The area was muddy from the heavy downpour and the overflowing pond, and he was cautious as he moved through the sticky ground.

Using his stick to probe the surface, he noticed a shiny reflection beneath the mud. His heart raced as he quickly bent down and began to dig with his hands. To his astonishment, he uncovered a shiny diamond, though it seemed tiny at first. As he continued to excavate, he realized it was a remarkable find, two centimeters long, the largest diamond discovered in the town so far.

That day, his courage outshone the diamond he discovered. He reflected on how fear had tried to overwhelm him at every stage, forcing him to give up, blame himself, and feel defeated. Yet, it was the courage to persist and try again, just one more time, that led him to the greatest success he had ever imagined. The diamond he found was not just a prize but a testament to the power of resilience and bravery.

Courage is also about belief; you need courage to be hopeful. Cowards are always focused on the negative aspects of life. They're afraid of everything, afraid of losing because they're too consumed by the fear of potential outcomes, and afraid of winning because they're so anxious about losing that they can't even imagine enjoying their success. Even if they do win, they fear of losing what they've gained.

You might have encountered such people in your life, and everyone does at some point. Because, at times, we have all been those cowards ourselves.

Courage is essential for handling both wins and losses. It's about facing everything that comes your way, whether it's favorable or not.

You need courage to swim through a river with the current against you, and you need courage to swim through a river with the current flowing along with you. When the water flows against you, you might fear not reaching your destination and ending up back where you started. When the water flows with you, you might fear moving too quickly and missing your destination. Courage means swimming on, regardless of the current, with the hope of reaching your goal.

Hope is the foundation upon which the entire system of life is built. At some point, someone had a vision, hoped for a result, and took action to achieve it. When you see results from something done today, remember that someone else took that first step without knowing what would happen. While not every result is intentional, some may be accidental. Truly remarkable outcomes are never the result of chance. They come from actions fueled by hope and courage because you've to be courageous to be hopeful.

Thomas Edison envisioned a light bulb and set out to bring it to life using the knowledge and materials available to him. Imagine the courage it took to embark on such an experiment, driven by the hope of achieving something that humankind had never seen before. His relentless pursuit demonstrated the courage to act on a vision, despite the uncertainty and challenges.

Sometimes, when you take a different route home, fear can creep in. You might worry about whether you'll make it back and what you might encounter along the way. Even though you eventually return to your familiar home in your small town, the fear and uncertainty can still linger, causing you to lose hope.

Imagine the courageousness of a man who envisioned a material that didn't yet exist in the world, a vision that took shape in his mind and drove him to bring it into reality. Despite the absence of a clear path to success, he boarded on a journey filled with trials and errors, trying various filaments to make the light bulb illuminate. Each attempt was a step into the unknown, with the chances of success being slim, one in thousands. Yet, he did not succumb to fear. If he had feared the numerous failures and given up after just ten or a hundred attempts, the world might still be enveloped in darkness. His unyielding belief in his vision, his dream, and his refusal to let fear dictate his actions are what ultimately lit up the world.

If he had been paralyzed by fear, he would have given up after trying ten filament materials, or even a hundred. But Edison's perseverance shone through. He succeeded only after testing ten thousand different filament materials before finally inventing the light bulb, transforming his dream into reality. His courage lay in his ability to hope despite repeated failures. Each failure was not a setback but a lesson, reinforcing his belief that the right material was still out there, waiting to be discovered. His relentless pursuit and refusal to let fear overshadow his vision are what ultimately illuminated the world.

That's what success is all about. That's how people win. They win by not giving up and by holding onto hope. The world operates on hope. We go to sleep tonight with the expectation that we'll wake up tomorrow. Every vacation you plan, every dream you pursue, every outfit you buy, every birthday you celebrate, every goal you chase is tied to something that will happen, something that is about to happen, or something that hasn't happened yet. Why do you do this? Because you're hopeful. You're hopeful for tomorrow, so you can sleep peacefully tonight. If you were told that the Earth would shatter tomorrow, you wouldn't be able to sleep for a single minute.

"To live without hope is to cease to live," he said.

"Isn't it amazing, Grandpa? To be so hopeful can sometimes seem a bit lunatic," I said.

He replied, "Indeed, sometimes the most unconventional thinkers come up with the most groundbreaking discoveries and success stories. But remember, not every eccentric person finds success. You can't be recklessly courageous or hopeful about trivial things. There has to be a balance, a purpose, and a focus in your courage and hope."

"I get it, but you must be lucky sometimes," I said.

He nodded and replied, "Indeed, fortune favors the bold."

"Courage and hope are crucial for winning, but so are hard work and determination," he explained. "You can't simply rely on courage and hope for things to unfold by themselves. Edison was indeed courageous, but he didn't just hope that the right filament would come to him. He tested ten thousand filaments. If he had merely hoped that the filament, he picked on a random Friday night would work, that would have been chasing luck. Instead, he worked tirelessly and tried ten thousand filaments before finally succeeding."

"Fortune favors the bold, the bold who never give up, who conquer their fears, and who put in their all. If you

want to get lucky, try every day. By trying every day, you'll never miss out on a lucky day."

There were two friends who were chasing their dream of becoming actors. They met each other at a film studio and bonded over their shared passion for filmmaking and acting. To cut down on living costs until they made it big, they decided to share both their goals and their apartment.

Every day, they woke up and dedicated themselves to contacting multiple film firms and production houses, all in search of new talent. Their routine consisted of sending emails, making phone calls, and submitting portfolios. They tirelessly attended auditions, hoping that each new opportunity would bring them closer to their dream.

One of them was relentless in his pursuit, determined never to miss a single day of trying. He was extraordinarily hopeful about landing a role in a film someday and truly believed in his success. He was so focused on his dream that he never allowed himself to fear the possibility of failure.

Sometimes, as they crossed busy streets near the film studios, famous actors would pass by in their luxurious cars. Without a hint of doubt, he would comment, "I'll have a car like that someday, just in a different color." His unwavering confidence and optimism were a proof to his deep belief in his own future success.

He once lost money to a fraudulent producer who promised him a role. Despite the setback, he said, "That's okay; I'll earn a thousand times to that amount once I become an actor, and I'll find and jail him then." He remained resolute in his belief that he would make it, no matter what.

While the other friend was also passionate, he was plagued by a constant fear of time slipping away and the uncertain lifestyle he was living. He would force himself to believe that he might get a chance to become an actor, despite facing multiple rejections and receiving no calls.

He gradually began to build a plan B for himself, preparing an alternative route in case his dream of acting did not materialize. He started investing time in his plan B while still trying to balance it with his efforts in plan A, acting.

The courageous one didn't pursue a plan B. While this made him seem risky and possibly reckless, he chose to fully commit to his dream. He embraced the uncertainty with boldness, believing that his courage and dedication would eventually lead him to success.

Every day, their routine repeated: they visited film shoots, production houses, and auditions, continually testing their work and luck. Despite their efforts, they faced failure repeatedly.

One day, the courageous one woke up and discovered that there was a shooting at a famous studio nearby. He decided to go there and seek his chance, just like he did every other day.

When he mentioned this to the fearful one, the response was, "There's nothing new that will happen. I've got other things to attend to. I've been to that studio for more than eight months and have never been given a chance. I'm afraid it will be the same today," and he chose to skip it.

While the courageous one went to the studio, he started shouting and cheering for the famous actor at the shooting spot, trying to get noticed. His enthusiasm caught the actor's attention, and the actor called him over to ask what he wanted.

The courageous one replied, "An autograph and a chance to prove my acting skills."

The actor, intrigued, asked, "Can you act?"

The courageous one took a deep breath and began to enact a famous scene from the actor's movie. He seamlessly switched between the roles of the protagonist and antagonist, delivering the dialogues with perfect precision and emotion. His performance was flawless, captivating everyone around him, including the actor.

Spellbound by the performance, the famous actor immediately instructed the producer to jot down the courageous one's details. He requested a personal audition right away and arranged for him to be signed for a movie role on the spot.

The courageous man leaped with joy, expressing his deep gratitude. He returned home, not with a sense of pride, but with a profound sense of accomplishment and hope fulfilled.

To the world, he appeared lucky. Fortune favored him, but it was his boldness that truly set him apart. He remained courageous and hopeful, never missing a day in his pursuit of his dream. He practiced tirelessly, refused to give up, and even had the audacity to scream for an autograph and a chance. His boldness drove him to chase what he wanted without fear, and that's why he won. That's what courage does to you, courage has multiple definitions, all of them are right in their own way and places. However, if they all collate together at one point, it would ask you to keep going, keep trying without being stagnant at tough times, situations, or battles.

I wish I expressed my feelings.

The next one. This is amusing; I wish I had expressed my feelings! As soon as my grandpa said this, I braced myself for a story from his youth, perhaps a love affair he once had. I couldn't help but smile.

He realized it immediately and added, "It's not what you think. Your grandmother is the only dear woman in my entire life. My generation was old-fashioned enough not to entertain such notions, unlike yours today."

"Then, what did you not express, and to whom?" I asked him.

"A few feelings, words, and emotions," he replied. "If I hadn't held back and shared what I truly felt at certain moments, it could have altered the course of my life and others' lives as well. It might have led to different outcomes than what actually happened."

"Like a domino effect?" I questioned.

"Ha-ha, yes! Something like that," he said.

Feelings are emotional reactions. A feeling is always a reaction; it can't be anything else. Whether you're hungry, angry, sad, dull, stressed, jovial, loved, or experiencing any of the countless other emotions, these feelings are responses to an event or situation. The event could be real or abstract, it doesn't matter!

"You think about someone you love," he continued, "like when I think about your grandmother, my eyes well up. I feel loved, and I fear leaving her alone." He wiped his eyes.

"Why have you made up your mind, Grandpa? The doctors will operate successfully," I said, trying to keep my emotions in check.

He smiled and continued, When God made our sensory perceptions, it's through them that we experience feelings. Sometimes, these emotions arise unexpectedly. At the same time, we must also have control over our reactions. Feeling something is a sign of a well-functioning body and mind, but extremes, whether high or low, are not ideal.

I've remained stoic for most of my life, he said. Being stoic doesn't mean not having feelings; it means being less expressive or reactive to them. It's about managing the feelings that hinder life and accepting what cannot be changed. When my brother died, I understood that he was gone forever. That realization both triggered and subdued my grief and acceptance. I was heartbroken, but I knew he couldn't be brought back, no matter what. I pushed my emotions aside that day. Similarly, I often withheld my feelings, and it became a habit. Now, there are countless emotions inside me, and I regret not letting most of them out.

"When you have a feeling that works against you, you never fail to embrace it. But when you experience something that points toward a positive outcome, you often barely acknowledge it. Why is that?"

"Yeah, you talk like you know me very well, Grandpa!" I said, relating to his insight.

"Most of us are the same, aren't we? After all, we're all human," he replied.

When my brother offered me a cigar for the first time, I had no desire to take it. Every cell in my body rejected it. I wanted to express that to him. I should have said, 'No! I don't want to smoke, nor will I ever give in to the habit you've taken up. I also want you to quit before it's too late and leads to health complications.' Instead, I just said, 'OK.'

If I had dared to express myself that day, I might never have smoked at all. Now, while I don't regret smoking too much, it was a companion through both good and bad times, a part of countless conversations, and a source of many of my ideas, I still wish I had avoided starting it. Maybe I'd be healthier now, with one less regret to share. But then, we wouldn't be having this conversation from my deathbed.

Even if my brother had listened to me, as I like to imagine, he might have stopped smoking too. Maybe he wouldn't have passed away so early, and I wouldn't miss him as profoundly as I do now.

Nevertheless, he is gone. Remember to express yourself. It's not necessary to do so every single time or for every feeling you have toward someone. Express when you should, when you want to, and when you must.

"Express when you must and when you want to, whether it's about someone or something that shapes your opinion. Just be wise about what's essential and when to speak up."

I remember a small incident when I first started as a teacher in my early career stage. All the teachers would gather for lunch in the dining area. Out of them, there was one known for his storytelling, another for his strict discipline, and one for his exceptional subject knowledge from the group.

I was having lunch with a colleague when this trio came in. They began sharing their perspectives on the best ways to teach students and what they considered the most essential elements of imparting knowledge.

The storyteller said that everything should be taught through stories. He believed that since students' brains are creative at that stage, relating concepts to a story would help them learn and retain the most.

The disciplinarian said that discipline is crucial for a student's success. Without it, students will eventually fail. He believed that teachers must instill discipline in students' lives for them to excel academically.

The knowledgeable teacher said that a teacher's expertise is crucial for learning. If a teacher lacks strong knowledge of the subject, how can students benefit from their instruction?

Their debate was so clear and loud that most of the teachers in the dining area could hear them. While each perspective had its merits, I believed that forming an emotional connection with students was most important. If you're emotionally invested in their growth, you'll be empathetic to their unique learning needs. Some students may benefit from stories, others from discipline, and some from a lot of questions answered. Ultimately, if you're not emotionally invested and students don't feel connected to you, everything will seem artificial. Students are perceptive and tend to ignore teachings that don't resonate with them emotionally.

I wanted to voice my thoughts, but I hesitated. I feared rejection, embarrassment, and judgment. So, I took another bite of my food and chewed slowly, pretending I hadn't heard their discussion.

Time passed, and the debate didn't resurface in the dining hall, except for one day: the school's annual day. The trio decided to bring up the topic with a renowned writer on pedagogy who attended as a guest to the event. When they posed their question in front of thousands of teachers and students, guess what the famous writer said?

"Emotion is the most important?!" I asked Grandpa.

Yes, he said exactly what I had thought but refrained from expressing. However, as a writer, he had his own way of articulating it and recited a poem he wrote

"In classrooms of facts and strict, rigid rules, where grades are the goal and teachers are fools, they miss what ignites a true spark in the mind, It's heart over knowledge that's one of a kind. So, forget the dry lessons and all of the drills, A bond's worth much more; it's connection that thrills. For while facts may fade, and stories may tire, it's love and emotions in the classroom that truly inspires."

However, it was the same conclusion I had reached. Everyone else was deeply impressed and began cheering for him.

When I say I regret not expressing myself, I don't just mean this particular situation, but rather in general. I failed to express myself at many other events and moments throughout my life.

You must develop the ability to say "No" and "Yes" without fear of judgment.

"Grandpa, you shouldn't regret this so much. I've expressed myself many times and ended up regretting it. I have my own share of embarrassments," I said.

"You might feel embarrassed when your words don't make sense. Your expressions are often just a combination of words, choose them wisely next time. Also, ensure you express them at the wise time and place. Everything matters. If you fail in this, you'll learn the opposite of what I'm teaching now and end up regretting your expressions."

Imagine you have a bow and an arrow in your hand, and your goal is to shoot an apple on a tree ten meters ahead. Your shot represents your expression. If you carefully observe the target, aim sharply, choose a pointed arrow and a strong bow, and release with precision, you'll hit the mark. That's how an effective expression yields results, literally and figuratively!

Having everything perfect but not taking the shot out of fear of missing it is not truly expressing yourself, you won't hit the mark or make an impact. Don't hold back. When you have the right words and timing, take your shot and make your voice heard.

Shooting the arrow at an old lady passing by instead of the apple is choosing the wrong situation and place to express yourself.

Using a blunt arrow and a weak bow to shoot at the apple is like using unwise words to express yourself.

Not holding something in your hand is like not feeling anything.

You decide what to do and what not to do. You won't always
find the perfect bow and arrow, nor will you always hit the
target. It's all part of the experience and learning process.
Sometimes, it's better to take a shot, even if it's not perfect,
rather than holding back and never using your skills.

Sometimes, before your arrow reaches the apple, other ar-
rows might shoot it down, people around you might have
expressed themselves more wisely.

**"It's better to take your shot and risk embarrassment
rather than not shooting at all. If you aim at a hanging
apple on a tree, the probability of hitting it is 50%. But if
you don't shoot, the probability is 0%."**

In a town far from the city and its sophisticated life, there
lived a family with two children and their parents. The two
brothers were quite different: the younger one was quiet and
rarely spoke to friends, while the elder was outspoken and
expressed his feelings openly, often without concern for the
consequences.

The elder brother's outspoken nature and his willingness to
express himself, despite potential judgment, earned him many
friends and some enemies. His family valued his words and
decisions, as he always shared his feelings and ideas, nurturing
a culture of open communication within the family and
friends.

Though his instinctive expression of feelings often brought him trouble, he still managed to navigate through those challenges.

In contrast, the younger brother rarely expressed himself. He seldom shared his feelings unless directly asked, often responding with just a word or two. This left other wondering and sometimes doubting what he truly felt.

This lack of expression created a distance within the family. Because he rarely shared his ideas, feelings, and emotions, they often went unheard. Despite their parents' and friends' efforts to encourage him to be more expressive, they failed, as they believed true expression must come from within. Even though he was still young, he would only become more outspoken and open when he felt a genuine need to do so, not through external influences.

Eventually, the family and friends grew tired of his inability to express himself and gave up trying. Instead of questioning or understanding his reluctance, they accepted it as a flaw and continued to live with it.

This led to a growing distance between him and his family and friends, straining their emotional connections and relationships. Over time, he became increasingly isolated, rarely speaking and spending much of his time alone.

One day, he met a new English teacher at school. The teacher noticed the boy's lack of expression deand asked if something was wrong. When the boy remained silent, his friend, who sat beside him, explained that he rarely spoke in class. The friend also mentioned that his family was aware of this issue but had grown indifferent to it over time.

Surprised, the teacher was determined to understand why the boy was so inexpressive and began to pay closer attention to him. He observed the boy during sports, other classes, and even looked into his studying and reading skills, but found no apparent issues.

One day, during a math lecture, the teacher noticed the boy attentively listening to the class. Curious, he stood outside the classroom, trying to peek through the window to gain insight into the boy's behavior.

As the lecture became more intense and the teacher wrote complex math problems on the board, the class started to ask numerous questions, clearly confused by what was happening on the blackboard.

As the students asked their questions, the English teacher noticed the young boy writing something on colored paper and slipping it into his bag. This happened several times, piquing the teacher's curiosity about what was written on those pieces of paper.

After the Math class, the English teacher asked the young boy to follow him to his office. Once there, he gently requested to see the boy's bag. The boy's eyes widened in fear, and though he wanted to refuse, he couldn't bring himself to express his feelings.

Noticing the boy's fear, the teacher tried to calm him down. He assured the boy that this wasn't a punishment and that he was simply interested in the bag. Slowly, he took the bag from the boy's hand, even as the boy continued to hesitantly resist.

As the English teacher took the bag, he noticed it contained several folded colored papers. Gently, he pulled them out and asked the boy, "What are these papers, kid? Do you like to write on them? Are they personal? Can I read them?"

The boy remained silent, offering neither approval nor rejection. The teacher reassured him, "Alright, I'll just read a few. Don't worry, I won't share your secrets with anyone."

As the teacher unfolded each paper, he was surprised by what he found. Each sheet contained the boy's thoughts, ideas, and feelings, everything he had kept inside, including questions from the last Math class that he hadn't asked. The teacher began to read through them one by one.

Paper 1: "If you have a fraction like 3/4, and you multiply it by a number, how can you figure out what happens to the size of the fraction compared to the original?"

Paper 2: "Dear brother, I've always wanted to tell you how much I respect you for who you are. I aspire to be like you someday, able to express myself without fear of rejection."

Paper 3: "Dear Dad, you've been distant lately. I know you tried to change me, but you gave up too easily, while I haven't given up. If I succeed someday, I'll tell you how much I want to talk to you every day."

Paper 4: "Dear Mom, I was waiting for you to ask me how was the lunch today. I enjoyed it a lot and hoped you'd cook it again for me. I know I could have told you myself, but I'm used to not speaking up. So, I wrote it here: I loved your food. It was tasty."

Paper 5: "Sir, you're the only one who tried to talk to me, understand me, and show kindness by trying to figure out what's wrong. I can't thank you enough for caring so much."

Paper 6: "When I was a kid, I tried to express myself but was often unheard. Sometimes my opinions were rejected, laughed at and other times I was suppressed. This had a major impact on me, and I stopped expressing myself. Even though I want to, I find it hard to do so now."

Paper 7: "It's not a great task, but only I know what I feel, and I can't voice it. I'm used to not reacting, venting, talking, or sharing. Only a miracle might help me break out of this endless loop."

As the teacher continued reading, he discovered more and more papers, each filled with the boy's inner thoughts. The teacher was astonished and deeply moved. Instead of blaming the boy, he sought to understand his feelings without making him feel bad or foolish.

He smiled and said, "You've expressed yourself well here. Expression isn't always about talking; it can also be through writing, art, music, or drawing. I understand that you can't always capture every word through other forms, which is why talking is often the best method. Still, your expression is very much alive through these papers."

"The fear of judgment is something we all face, worrying about what others will think of our opinions and ideas. But remember, people will eventually forget them, whether they're good or bad. If not now, then later. You shouldn't let this fear hold you back. It's better to be disagreed with than to remain unheard."

Now, here's what I want you to do: take these old papers and set them aside. Instead, write on five new papers about what you want to express to five different people, whoever they may be. Then, give those papers to them.

The kid hesitated, shaking his head. The teacher said, "Alright, start with me. I'll take the privilege of being one of those five people. I promise not to judge you. Write something for me and give it to me when you're ready."

The kid took a moment, then handed over Paper 5 to the teacher. The teacher, noticing the paper, asked with a smile, "Is this for me?" The kid responded with a grin, "Yes!"

The teacher read the note aloud with enthusiasm and a smile, clearly delighted by the words. He showed his agreement and appreciation, making the moment both warm and affirming for the kid.

After reading it out loud, the teacher said, "Thank you. It's my pleasure. You're very expressive with your words; I'm sure people would love to hear what you have to say." The kid bent his head, showing no outward emotion, but deep down, he felt a spark of newfound confidence.

The teacher said, "Alright, that's it for today. Let's plan a new letter tomorrow." The kid, filled with joy and a newfound sense of bravery, ran off, his heart overflowing with excitement and determination.

The next day, the teacher entered the classroom and announced, "Class, we're having an English spelling test. The details will be written on the board." Then, he called the kid to the front of the class and said softly, "You don't have to say anything, just write what I tell you on the board."

The kid was initially shocked but felt a sense of calm, as he only had to write rather than speak. The English teacher guided him through writing, erasing, and rewriting until the boy had neatly recorded the details of an upcoming competition two weeks away.

Gradually, the teacher encouraged him to distribute letters to friends, his brother, and his family. Over time, the kid overcame his fear of expressing his feelings and confidently handed out the letters, no longer worried about judgment. He began writing poems and short stories based on his experiences, sharing them on the school wall. When people read and complimented his work, he would smile, genuinely pleased with how things were turning out.

Feeling a surge of confidence, he decided to speak to the English teacher. He entered the office, pulled out a long letter he had written, and began reading it aloud. In the letter, he expressed his deep gratitude, detailing how the teacher had transformed his life and helped him find his voice.

At first, the boy was nervous, but the teacher, acting as if he hadn't noticed, offered gentle support, encouraging him to express himself. Over the following months, the teacher observed a remarkable change in the boy's behavior. He began expressing himself through all emotions, politely, confidently, strongly, and respectfully, depending on the situation. He successfully rebuilt his relationships with friends and family, regaining both his emotional voice and his connections.

When the teacher returned to the school after a few years, he saw that the once-reserved boy had become the leader of the student association, poised to graduate.

"That's fantastic, Grandpa! It's wonderful to hear about such inspiring teachers," I exclaimed with joy, captivated by the story.

Curious, I asked, "Where did this take place? Do you know who that student was?"

With a proud smile, my grandpa replied, "The teacher was me, and that student is now a famous writer."

I wasn't surprised. I knew my grandpa well. He had a knack for performing miracles.

"I'm not surprised, Grandpa! You've always had the ability to change people's lives."

"I have the potential to be a great teacher because I was once in the same situation as that student. I faced similar challenges, though I didn't write my thoughts down. Instead, I kept them to myself and shared them only with my best friend a few times. I didn't express myself much."

That student, who later became a famous writer, dedicated a book to me called 'The Forgotten Thought'.

In it, he captured a conversation between two people, Jim and David, expressing their innermost thoughts and feelings.

Jim: Why is it necessary to express ourselves?

David: Why not? Expression is the first step towards action. To move forward and make progress, you must first express your thoughts and feelings.

Jim: I don't want to contribute to the world's progress. Should I remain inexpressive?

David: Who says every expression leads to progress around you? You're not required to see yourself as a great influencer. Instead, it's important to focus on your own growth. Your expression is primarily for your own progression.

Jim: How is that possible?

David: What do you want to do today?

Jim: Read.

David: Read, what?

Jim: Humor.

David: Read the "Sixty Jokes by Uncle Tom". I read it last week, and it's fantastic. I'll give you, my copy.

Jim: Awesome, I'll do that.

David: This is why you've to express. Reading is your form of execution. Choosing the genre and book is part of the plan, but expressing your plan made the execution easier. You'll progress by reading, laughing, and finding joy and accomplishment.

Jim: Does this apply everywhere?

David: Mostly, yes. Unless you're expressing very personal or offensive feelings, you're unlikely to get into trouble. Your expression states your thoughts, people around who resonates might help you, join you and make your journey easier, if people don't resonate, they might debate, argue and find mistakes which would help you after all. Or sometimes, your expressions might just get your wants. Expression is to express, if you're inexpressive, you're unconsidered everywhere you go.

Jim: What happens if I'm not expressive?

David: If you don't express yourself, you miss out on understanding who you are. Your expressions are the building blocks of your character, personality, and traits. Without sharing your views with others or even yourself, you're like water that simply takes the shape of its container.

Jim: How do I overcome the fear of judgment and rejection of my expressions?

David: By facing judgment and rejection.

Jim: What?

David: Sometimes, to understand what lies in the darkness, you must enter it. You only truly learn what it means to be judged or rejected by experiencing it yourself. Rejections and judgments aren't always setbacks; they help you understand, correct, rethink, and reconstruct your feelings, emotions, ideas, and thoughts. Don't fear rejection, embrace it and try again. The real fear isn't judgment or rejection, but being unheard and not considered.

Jim: How do I deal with the regret of being inexpressive?

David: To overcome regret, you need to stop wasting time and start expressing yourself. Regret is tied to things that have already happened. Once something has occurred, dwelling on it isn't productive, regret should be a fleeting feeling. Learn from your mistakes, make new ones, learn again, and keep working. That's the path to improvement.

Expression isn't a one-time effort; it's a continuous loop of stages and revisions. Not every thought, idea, or feeling is perfect from the start. It begins as a spark and undergoes multiple iterations to achieve clarity.

Sometimes, we engage in a lot of self-talk when we find ourselves in difficult situations, whether it's to motivate ourselves, place blame, express anger, or rationalize our actions. For instance, after I slapped a friend in a moment of anger during a fight, regret set in quickly. I found myself explaining my actions to myself, telling myself it was understandable given what he had said about me.

Imagine using self-talk to shift how you feel about something or someone. When I met him again and he made the same comments, I told myself to let it go, he wasn't worth the fight. If I hadn't talked myself down, I might have ended up in another confrontation.

Why do we often expect others to understand us without explaining ourselves to them, even though we take the time to explain things to ourselves?

In the early days of my job, I was intimidated by my superiors. I would work hard and often stay late, helping them or taking on additional tasks. Whenever I tried to avoid extra work, I found myself assigned even more the next day. It wasn't that they were being mean; it was just a reflection of their expectations of a junior. Over time, things changed.

However, I had your grandmother and my children to look after. I didn't want to risk their well-being by outright revolting against my superiors, so I would extend my work into the late hours to manage both my responsibilities and their expectations.

When this continued for several days, your grandmother confronted me, asking if I could come home earlier and spend more time with the family. I didn't want to disclose all the details about my office situation, so I simply told her I had a lot of work and couldn't compromise on it.

I didn't share the details of what was happening at work because I didn't want her to feel bad for me or worry. I didn't want to risk losing my job and making her suffer. Instead, I chose to work even harder so that she wouldn't have to worry as much. That's how I showed my love for her.

One evening, everything changed. She told me I was an irresponsible father and husband who cared more about my friends at work than about my family. I was furious. I replied, "Yes, it is what it is. Think what you want, and I won't say another word."

I sat there, fuming, and said to myself, "How could she possibly understand what I'm going through for the sake of our family? Does she even realize how hard it is for me? It's okay if she doesn't understand; that's her loss. I'm not going to explain what's happening."

This continued for a while until things eventually settled back to normal, and she seemed to forget what she had said. One day, I was struck by the urge to explain, so I told her what had actually been happening and why I used to stay late at work, despite completing my own tasks on time.

She replied, "Why didn't you tell me? I would have supported you and might have even suggested ways to get out of that situation."

I said, "I thought you understood and supported me. You must know how hard I worked for you and the kids. When you thought otherwise, I was disappointed."

She then said, "Until you express yourself, how could I possibly understand what's happening inside you?"

Her words struck me hard. I realized that while I was talking to myself to ease my frustration, I had no right to expect her to understand what I was going through without actually sharing it with her.

I wish I didn't Procrastinate.

There was a frog that rested on a big lotus leaf, where it spent all day sleeping. It used its long, sticky tongue to catch flies and insects that came by, chewing them slowly before swallowing them. The frog rarely moved or explored the pond, content to stay on its one big leaf.

One day, a crocodile came from a larger lake swam into the pond, eating everything in its way. When it approached the frog, the frog tried to jump from the leaf to the shore. But it didn't succeed.

It fell into the pond and was quickly eaten by the crocodile.

The frog had always told itself, "Tomorrow." Don't be that frog. There is no tomorrow.

Tomorrow is abstract. It doesn't exist. It never comes to you, when you sleep tonight and wake up the tomorrow is not found. Only 'Today' is found. Don't sleep countless nights waiting for that tomorrow. It doesn't exist. All you have is Today. Not even yesterday.

That's my next regret: I wish I had avoided procrastination. Speed is crucial. You need to be able to act quickly. Yet, nowadays, people are taking longer than necessary to get things done. I've procrastinated in my life and regretted it, but now I worry about this generation. Many people struggle with focus and can't complete tasks on their own.

Never watch the clock when you have something to do. Just do it. Don't wait for the "right time" to start; it won't help and will only delay your task further.

At every stage of my life, I procrastinated at times, leading to unchangeable events and deep regrets. There's nothing I can do about it now, except share with you and others on how not to waste your precious time and opportunities.

Was I unaware of the consequences of procrastination? Yes, I was fully aware, as are those who struggle with it. Yet, they still procrastinate. Why?

I asked myself the same question and found the answer. Many people procrastinate because they believe, "We still have time." In reality, time is slipping away faster than they realize. For your generation, time seems to pass more quickly. The days and nights fly by, and before you know it, you'll be an adult and then an old person lying in bed. Technology and the demands of modern life have made time feel even more fleeting when you spend yourself scrolling on social media consuming content and let it consume you later.

So, the idea that you have plenty of time left is a misconception. In reality, the time you have is much less than you think. You need to take action now.

Let me tell you my own story of procrastination, when I was a teenager, my father urged me to join an internal youth group in our town. This group was involved in activities like physical fitness, exercising, assisting organizations in need, and supporting government authorities and events. Members of this group were highly respected and enjoyed privileges, including easier access to government jobs.

My father was determined for me to join this group in town. One day, he practically dragged me there and asked the coach, who was a friend of his, to let me join. The coach agreed, and on my first day, I was put through push-ups, pull-ups, squats, and sprints. I was exhausted by the end and vowed never to go back. But fate had other plans; my father brought me there again the next day, and it became a routine. Though I eventually got used to it, I never really enjoyed it. I always longed to escape and spend my evenings with friends at the riverside, chatting about our lives.

After a few days, I was chatting with a friend from the troop. He asked why I always seemed so unhappy when I arrived and whether I really wanted to be a part of it. I shared my perspective and explained what I would have done if I hadn't joined the group.

He laughed and said, "I was just like you when I first joined, but I became disciplined. Let me share my routine with you. Try following it; it will definitely help."

The routine included food, exercise, and various daily activities designed to keep me fit both physically and mentally, with the aim of motivating me to join the troop each day. I looked at it and thought to myself, "I don't want to be part of this group all day long, and now my friend is making it seem like I'm committed for the entire day."

I told my father I didn't want to continue and that I was really hating it. He responded emotionally, saying, "Look at our family's situation. We need you to succeed and earn well so you can help improve our lives. Right now, it's tough for you to even land a low-paying job. This troop is closely connected with the government. If you stick with it, you'll be recognized eventually and have the chance to get a good job. It's hard now, but it will pay off in the end, and I'll be proud of you."

Inspired by my father's words, I decided I would commit to it. I took out the paper chart my friend had given me and went to sleep, planning to wake up early the next day to start my exercise routine.

When I woke up, it was winter, cloudy, and foggy outside. I looked at the old, torn blanket covering me. We couldn't afford a new one, and I thought this was my chance to improve our situation. I glanced at the clock and thought, "I have some time," and went back to sleep. I didn't wake up again until four hours later when the sun was shining brightly.

I kept telling myself, "Tomorrow." And each time, I ended up sleeping in.

One day, I finally got up and went for a run. I felt good and thought, "Maybe this isn't so bad. Perhaps I'll come to like it." I continued the next day, but on the third day, I slept in again. I skipped the fourth day too and went for a run on the fifth day, thinking it might be my last chance. After that, I never went back to the troop or went for a walk again.

Two years later, a major protest broke out in town over a government policy, causing significant disruption. Some protestors even tried to burn down a huge rice mill in the town. When the mill was set on fire, the troop sprang into action to help. They quickly organized and managed to rescue fourteen people trapped inside the building. I watched them from a distance, amazed. All the push-ups, pull-ups, sprints, and squats they had trained for were put to use that day, and I saw firsthand how their training made a real difference in the rescue effort.

The government recognized the troop's bravery and, within a year, awarded them jobs in various sectors with special consideration, including exemptions from some tests for certain positions.

I was frustrated and angry with myself, and I felt a deep sense of regret for my father. I went home, pulled the same torn blanket over me, and tried to sleep. I spent many days under that blanket, avoiding action due to my procrastination. But when the regret hit me, I found I couldn't even sleep under that old blanket for the next few months.

What makes it hard for us to act at the right time? It could be that we don't like what we need to do, we like it but find it difficult, we're unsure of how to do it, we're doing it for someone else, or we enjoy it but are simply too lazy. Despite of any reasons one might have, the final question would be only if the task was done or not?

Laziness is regret in disguise. It might seem rewarding at first, but it eventually turns into regret, much stronger and more painful than we anticipated.

Once, in an apartment building, there were two neighbors living next to each other. The garbage van came once every three days to collect the trash. One neighbor consistently took out the trash on time and handed it over to the truck, keeping his house and surroundings clean. The other neighbor was lazy and kept telling himself, "Maybe next time."

As a result, the diligent neighbor maintained a clean home and a pleasant environment, while the lazy neighbor's house and corridor became increasingly filthy and filled with a terrible smell.

This went on for days, and before trash piled up around his house, the smell filled the entire apartment, and he ended up falling sick. Not only that, but the apartment committee evicted him from the building, leaving the mess behind.

"Can you guess how many weeks the tenant didn't take out the trash?" my grandpa asked me.

"Maybe around fifteen weeks?" I guessed, uncertain.

My grandpa laughed and said, "Ha-ha, just four weeks. That's eight bins of trash. It was enough to make the whole house stink and eventually make him sick."

When I asked you how many weeks, you guessed fifteen. That's how people often think, that there's always more time. That's how the tenant thought, too. He believed he had plenty of time, but in reality, he had no more than a week.

You might argue that not everything needs to be done immediately, and that's true, everything has its own time. But did you do what is needed to be done today? If you didn't, you probably have less time than you think and might end up falling behind. If you don't take action now, you might find yourself in a situation where things go wrong, just like the tenant with the trash.

Action prevents regret. If you're unhappy with your current situation, you need to take action. Regret often comes from not taking the right steps.

Action can help clear confusion and combat depression. Even if you don't achieve the results you hoped for, you'll face less regret than if you hadn't tried at all.

Imagine losing after giving your best effort versus losing without trying. You'd feel better knowing you gave it your all. Trying isn't just about doing something for the sake of it; it's about putting in your best effort. If you think otherwise, you're just finding excuses not to work.

If you truly give your best, you're more likely to achieve what you want. Also, avoid making excuses. Sometimes, when you share your dreams, people might doubt you. While you shouldn't let their judgments determine your path, remember that not every piece of feedback is wrong. Evaluate it and use it to guide your efforts.

Treat it as constructive feedback and try to understand why they might not believe in your dreams. Is it due to their perception of your goals, or perhaps because they know you well and have concerns based on that? Use their feedback to reflect on your approach and make necessary adjustments.

Words alone aren't enough; actions determine your destination. You can talk for a hundred days, but an hour of action outweighs all those words. To gauge if someone can achieve their goals, pay attention to whether they have excuses. Excuses often reveal a lack of commitment or readiness to take action.

You should never look for excuses, even if you have countless opportunities to do so. The day you start finding excuses is the day you become stagnant. "I have no time," "I have a disease," "I have a problem", these are just endless excuses.

Those who truly want to achieve something focus on what needs to be done, what they can do right now, and what opportunities are available. They don't dwell on what they lack, what's missing, or why they don't have as much as someone else. Instead, they concentrate on taking action and making the most of what they have.

You need to start now and figure things out as you go. Waiting for the perfect conditions to begin will only hold you back. There will never be an ideal time to start; the purpose of starting is to work towards creating those ideal conditions.

If you wait for everything to be perfect, you'll never begin. Start now, and you'll eventually work your way to the conditions you're aiming for.

Two men set out to work in the deserts of Qatar. Each day, their job was to take camels into the desert and search for valuable pebbles. At the end of the day, they would return to their employer, a jewelry merchant, and hand over the pebbles they had collected. The merchant used these pebbles to create special necklaces, embedding them into designs crafted from the treasures found in the desolate desert.

Every day, both men embarked on their journey with camels, seeking out a small shelter made of tents. They would tie their camels to a large date tree, the only one in the barren land, and then begin their search for valuable pebbles.

Both men had immigrated from different countries and hoped to return home once they had earned enough to settle their debts. One of them never made excuses and consistently did what was required, regardless of the conditions around him. The other constantly sought ideal conditions to begin and found excuses for not starting, no matter what.

The merchant received a significant order from a customer who had previously bought one of his pebble necklaces. She loved it so much that she asked him to make hundred more for her family and friends. The merchant informed her that he would need some time to gather the necessary pebbles and assured her that he would complete the order as soon as possible.

The owner instructed both workers to search the desert for a week and bring back fifteen hundred stones. The workers were shocked; previously, they had only managed to collect about twenty stones each time they went out. The owner promised that the worker who collected the most stones would receive double the pay.

The disciplined worker was excited and envisioned himself finding the most stones and returning home with double the money. The other worker was also enthusiastic and loudly proclaimed that he would alone find a thousand stones and return to his country by clearing his debts after getting the double pay. The owner smiled and asked both of them to begin their search.

They both set out on their journey to the desert on their camels and arrived at a tent. The disciplined worker quickly tied his camel and immediately grabbed his large pouch, setting out to search for stones.

The other worker, however, told himself, "I've just crossed this vast desert. I should rest a bit so I can start searching with full energy." He slowly settled into the tent and fell asleep.

The disciplined worker continued his search aggressively and had found about thirty pebbles by the afternoon. When he returned to the tent to take a sip of water, the other worker asked, "How many did you find?"

"Just thirty," he replied.

"Thirty? That's it?" the other worker exclaimed.

The disciplined man simply smiled and nodded in agreement.

The worker who often made excuses told himself, "It's too sunny outside, and it looks like there aren't many pebbles here. The other guy only found thirty. I'll stay in the tent until the sun goes down and then search intensively in the last few hours of the day to surpass him." He ate the food he had brought along and continued his nap.

Meanwhile, the disciplined worker didn't worry about the sun or the heat. His only focus was to find enough pebbles to clear his debt. He drank two glasses of water, skipped lunch, and ventured out into the scorching heat.

Throughout the afternoon, he covered about five miles around the tent, finding just ten more pebbles. As the sun set and it began to get dark, he returned to the tent. Although he was disappointed with his total haul, he felt a sense of accomplishment for working hard.

The worker who made excuses was eating bananas in the tent and asked, "How many did you find?"

"Ten," the disciplined worker replied.

The excuses man thought to himself, "It's good I decided to skip the search today. It looks like there aren't many pebbles around here; he only found ten. I'll start fresh tomorrow at a different location."

Both men returned home on their camels as night fell. The next day, a massive desert storm rolled in. Despite the danger, the disciplined worker decided to risk it all and continued his search. Meanwhile, the other man quickly found a new excuse, he decided to skip the second day entirely due to the storm.

The storm caused the tent to blow away, leaving the disciplined worker without shelter. Undeterred, he pressed on. The storm had shifted the sand, bringing many pebbles to the surface. The disciplined worker worked tirelessly throughout the day and managed to find around three hundred pebbles by the end of the second day.

When the disciplined worker returned home, he was greeted by the other man, who asked, "How many did you find?"

With a huge smile on his face, the disciplined worker replied, "Three hundred."

The excuses man was shocked and asked, "How did you find so many all at once?"

"There was a huge storm," the disciplined worker explained. "The storm displaced the sand, and the pebbles were pushed to the surface."

"Where?" the other man asked, eager to know.

"Four miles east of our tent," he replied.

"Great!" the excuses man thought to himself. "I'll search there all day without resting and return home with at least five hundred pebbles."

After spending the entire day in the storm, the disciplined worker fell ill but resolved to continue working rather than resting.

The next day, they both set out on their journeys. The disciplined worker ventured ten miles further from the previous day's location, convinced that he would find more pebbles due to the effects of the storm. Meanwhile, the excuses man headed towards the spot where the other had previously found the pebbles, hoping to collect as many as he could.

The excuses man began his search but found few pebbles, as most of them had already been collected by the disciplined worker the previous day. After a few hours of searching, he managed to find only fifteen pebbles. Frustrated, he decided to return home before the day was half over.

Meanwhile, the disciplined worker endured the storm once more and managed to collect an additional two hundred pebbles. Despite his illness and the harsh conditions, he persevered and returned home with a significant haul.

The pattern continued for three more days until the week concluded, and it was time for both workers to present their collected pebbles to the owner.

The owner, curious and anxious about whether they had gathered enough stones, asked for the results. The excuses man listed all his complaints to the owner: the heat, the storm, tired camels, and his stomach ache, and many. At the end of his lengthy explanation, he handed over his pouch and said, "All I managed to find were seventy pebbles."

The disciplined man quietly opened his large pouch and presented it to the owner. "Here, I've collected over fifteen hundred pebbles," he said. He mentioned that he had been sick, hungry, faced harsh storms, and endured high heat, but he never gave up. He had committed to leaving no excuses and did his search on time, every day.

The owner was deeply impressed and extremely pleased with his dedication. True to his word, he awarded the disciplined man double the amount of pay. The worker used his earnings to take a long-awaited vacation, return home, clear his debts, and spend time with his family. Meanwhile, the excuses man continued to work twice as hard for the same wage over the next few months.

When one is genuinely determined to accomplish something, excuses fade into irrelevance. Conversely, the presence of excuses suggests a lack of true desire. Excuses, therefore, ought to serve as the impetus for action rather than justification for inaction.

Procrastination often occurs because we believe we have plenty of time. But in reality, time slips away quickly, and before we know it, years will pass. People usually don't take action until they are in a dire situation. When they finally do act, they often rush and become overwhelmed, leading to frustration and giving up because it's already too late.

Imagine a modern man placed inside a sealed glass chamber with no keys or tools available to escape. The chamber is automatically controlled and has a small pipe connected to it, allowing a slow but steady flow of water. The environment inside the chamber is comfortable, with a cool temperature and a cozy atmosphere.

To escape the chamber, he must solve a series of math puzzles displayed on a TV screen outside the chamber. While the setting is pleasant, the challenge lies in solving the puzzles correctly to find the way out before the water accumulates too much.

He must solve five hundred math questions correctly to pass the test and escape the chamber. If he answers a question incorrectly, it will be skipped and not counted. However, each incorrect answer increases the difficulty of the subsequent questions. The chamber will only open once he has correctly solved all five hundred puzzles.

Initially, he resists the urgency of the situation, believing that the slow water flow gives him ample time to work at his own pace. He starts by solving just two or three questions, then distracts himself by scrolling through social media on his phone. As he notices the water beginning to rise, he answers a few more questions but gets some incorrect. Believing he still has time, he takes a nap, convinced that the minimal water flow means he has plenty of time to solve the remaining puzzles.

He becomes too comfortable, taking naps in the cozy chamber, scrolling through his phone, watching movies, and occasionally solving a few puzzles before returning to his distractions. Over time, he loses track of how quickly the water level is rising while he's not focusing on what needs to be done. Eventually, he notices that the water has reached a distance up the chamber, made his bed damp and forcing him to stay awake and deal with the increasing urgency.

He glances at the TV and sees that he has only solved 24 out of 500 puzzles. Looking around the chamber, he notices that the water level has already reached one-fourth of the chamber's height. He tells himself, "Alright, I might have wasted some time, but it's only one-fourth filled. I'll start focusing now and solve the puzzles."

He then, with renewed determination, solves twenty more puzzles. However, as he starts answering a few incorrectly, he reaches for his phone, needing a break. Unable to sleep, he scrolls through social media instead. Despite knowing he's wasting valuable time and needing to get back to solving puzzles, he keeps telling himself he'll do it later.

Suddenly, he notices that the water has risen to halfway up the chamber. Realizing how much time he has wasted; he resolves to stop his distractions and focus entirely on solving the puzzles. He commits to solving them all in one go, taking no breaks, and continues working intensely to escape the chamber.

He manages to solve 120 out of 500 puzzles and tells himself, "It's about 100 questions straight, I answered. I need a small break," even though he's in deep trouble. He spends some time watching his phone, but soon starts to panic as the water level rises to his chest. In his panic, he throws his phone into the rising water and forces himself to work faster. He manages to solve 214 puzzles out of 500, but the water level continues to rise and reaches his neck.

The water level reaches his eyes, and he has solved 301 out of 500 puzzles. Immersed in water, he has to jump up each time to see the next puzzle on the display. Despite his desperate efforts, he manages to solve only 13 more puzzles, reaching a total of 315. Eventually, the water overwhelms him, and he succumbs to the rising flood, unable to continue.

Let's reflect on the mistakes made:

1. Taking breaks when you're not tired: Taking unnecessary breaks despite having ample time and energy led to wasted moments and delayed progress.

2. Constantly distracting yourself consciously but not taking action: Choosing to scroll through your phone and watch movies instead of focusing on solving the puzzles contributed to the delay and eventual crisis. Your brain seeks the same fun when you're away from it even for a while and will force you return to your pleasures.

3. Believing you've got time: Assuming that you had plenty of time led to procrastination, causing the water to rise uncontrollably as the deadline approached.

4. Not anticipating the problems that would come from the work undone today: Failing to recognize the accumulating consequences of incomplete work led to a critical shortage of time and a heightened sense of urgency.

5. Not working faster when the problems were not yet critical: Ignoring the need to accelerate efforts while the situation was still manageable resulted in a rushed and ineffective final attempt.

6. Not allocating time to review incorrect answers: Neglecting to address and correct mistakes meant that incorrect answers piled up, making the task more difficult and contributing to the overall failure.

To save himself from the chamber, the man needs to act quickly. He should allow himself to panic immediately after being placed inside. While panic, fear, and stress are usually harmful, if he doesn't panic at the start, he might become distracted and too calm, which could be dangerous. By panicking right away, he will be motivated to take action, which can help him manage his fear. If he waits until the end, when there's no more time to act, that panic and worry could lead to disaster.

Panic and start solving puzzles immediately. Take breaks only when you're truly exhausted, like when you're so tired you can't even read the question because your eyes won't stay open. Stay focused, avoid distractions like your phone, and keep working. Solve as many puzzles as you can, knowing that not every answer will be correct.

I realized my grandpa was not actually referring to a man locked in a chamber with his story and it was how I wasted time always scrolling my phone and wasting time, drawing myself to same pleasures without sense of urgency when something has to be done in my life. I realized his subtle way of warning me to be more focused and avoid procrastinating before it's too late and I continued to listen to him.

Life is designed to constantly challenge you with dreams, goals, and problems that need solving with minimal breaks and no procrastination. Why? Because the more time you waste, the more panic you'll face in the end, leading to failure and giving up.

You need to start taking action from day one. Approach your tasks with such urgency that others believe you're working on something with an immediate deadline. Only by working this way will you achieve something extraordinary and truly stand out.

That's why people who want to succeed and achieve greatness often appear stressed. However, this doesn't mean you should immerse yourself in stress and give up on happiness or joy. Instead, take inspiration from the understanding that the bigger your goals, the less time you'll have to achieve them. In an age full of distractions and opportunities to procrastinate, it's crucial to recognize the urgency of completing tasks within limited time.

In today's competitive world, you can't rely on old habits like working at your own pace, taking frequent breaks, or getting easily distracted. Your focus needs to be razor-sharp. What should be done today should have been completed yesterday, and what's planned for tomorrow should be finished today. By working with this kind of urgency, you outpace procrastination and overcome it.

To avoid procrastination, you need to keep moving forward. Start and finish tasks without delay. Only if you're exceptionally disciplined and focused can you afford a brief pause in between tasks.

Three types of Procrastinators according to my grandpa:

1. The Lethargic Procrastinators

These individuals know what needs to be done but don't do it because they are simply lazy. Laziness isn't a straightforward emotion; it's often the result of many past actions and thought patterns. Overcoming it is a challenging task that only a few manage to achieve. If someone is lazy, they might be aware of it and may try to address it, fail, or give up entirely without fully understanding why they struggle with it.

These individuals struggle to finish tasks on time, moving slowly, taking numerous breaks, and getting easily distracted. Their inability to focus means the chances of them achieving their goals successfully are essentially zero. In a competitive world where speed is crucial, moving at a sluggish pace won't help them succeed. They are likely to falter and fail, and even though they know their approach will lead to failure, they find themselves trapped in a cycle of procrastination, ultimately facing the consequences of their inaction.

2. The Egotistical Procrastinators

These individuals are too proud or stubborn to learn, correct mistakes, or acknowledge the need for improvement. Instead of focusing on their tasks, they spend their energy arguing and making excuses. They invest time and effort into justifying their lack of progress rather than addressing their work. If they directed their energy towards actual work rather than defending their inaction, they could achieve as much success as those who don't procrastinate.

When you talk to arrogant procrastinators, it's easy to identify them. For example, if you ask, "Hey! Why didn't you do this? It could benefit you," they might respond with, "I know what it could do for me, but I'm not interested," or "I already know it's of no use." They claim to know without having tried or tested it. Convincing them is nearly impossible, arguing with them is often more frustrating than dealing with the procrastination itself.

Or, they might wait for the perfect conditions or come up with excuses to delay starting the work. I always say that the easiest thing in the world is to criticize others, and next comes finding excuses. Excuses can be made for anything. Just name it, and I can come up with an excuse for it. My grandpa challenged me amid our conversation.

I said, "Grandpa, you'll be fine."

Grandpa replied, "The doctors at this hospital have a bad reputation; they won't successfully operate on me."

I said, "You should have stopped smoking; you wouldn't be in this bed now."

Grandpa replied, "I know plenty of people who smoked and are healthier than I am and will outlive me."

I said, "You should have worked out and gone to the gym to stay fit."

Grandpa replied, "Have you heard that a lot of people who go to the gym are having heart attacks these days?"

I said, "You should have invested money when you were younger; it would benefit you now."

Grandpa replied, "I'm happy with what I have. I don't regret not investing. I believe in spending rather than investing, and that approach has worked well for me."

I said, "You should eat healthy food to stay healthy."

Grandpa replied, "Not necessarily. I read about a woman in Korea who ate only junk food and lived to 117 years."

I said, "I can't, Grandpa! That's it."

Grandpa replied, "You can; you're just acting."

I said, "Stop kidding around, grandpa"

Grandpa replied, "Ha-ha, see? I told you, the easiest thing in the world is making excuses."

So, do they succeed, Grandpa? I asked.

He replied, "The lazy ones arrive at the destination after the winner is declared and the audience has gone home, while the arrogant ones don't even start the race. So, you know the answer."

3. The Ignorant Procrastinators

They procrastinate simply because they are unaware that they are doing so. Essentially, they don't realize they're in a race with a finish line to cross. Their lack of awareness means they don't see the urgency or importance of completing their tasks on time. They are like babies put on a race track. They just sleep, play or look at others cheering for them and laugh hard because they're unaware they've to race.

They are the ones who leave control of their lives to God or fate. However, neither God nor fate controls anyone's life. The only real control comes from one's own actions, thoughts, and desires. By relying entirely on external factors like God or fate, they abdicate their personal responsibility and control over their own lives.

They don't follow a set path; they go wherever they see fit at the moment. If the wind pushes them in another direction, they travel that way. The time it takes them to realize they've strayed and find their way back to their original path is the time they've spent procrastinating.

"So, you don't have to pray God for blessings?" I asked.

Grandpa replied "I'll just share my opinion. Your true actions and commitment are your actual prayers and the results are the blessings."

I wish I Forgave.

Forgiveness. They say, forgive but don't forget, but I forgot to forgive a few people in my life. This is one of my regrets.

We humans generally live by our own handbooks, shaped by our beliefs, principles, and expectations. Each of us roam around with our personal handbook, much like wearing colored sunglasses. Each pair of sunglasses has a unique tint, and some groups might share the same color. When someone with red-tinted glasses meets someone with yellow-tinted glasses, one sees the sun as yellow while the other sees it as red. They end up arguing under the shade of a tree not realizing the Sun is a blend of both red and yellow, Orange.

So, humans often operate in a way where, even when they're told that everyone wears different-colored sunglasses, they still argue their point. I was one of those people who, at times in my life, argued with others, regardless of who was right or at fault. I've since come to realize that we all see things differently, and I shouldn't be disappointed by that.

"I don't remember you ever getting angry at someone, Grandpa! Are there people in your life who really caused a disruption that you never forgave?" I asked, astonished.

"Yes, there are. I might not have expressed anger in the way you're familiar with, anger is a complex emotion. You might not have seen me yell or lose my temper, but that doesn't mean I don't get angry. My way of expressing anger is different. Sometimes I simply choose not to speak to someone, I disagree with them, I might humiliate them, or I might choose not to forgive them, and I even end up regretting it."

Every time I was furious and sparked an argument with friends, family members, or even strangers, I rarely took the initiative to talk, apologize, or forgive. I believed that doing so would make me appear weak or inferior, so I always hoped the other person would make the first move. However, as I've grown older, I've come to realize that with our lives being so limited and our time so fleeting, we barely have enough of it to spend with others. In that precious time, we do have, why should I waste it by not talking to or forgiving them?

Assuming I live for eighty years, if I count the total time spent with others, it would amount to hardly a year, two, or maybe three out of the whole lifetime, with the rest dedicated to myself. Given this limited time, why should I waste it by making relationships unpleasant, even for a short while? Even with strangers, if I have a conflict, I might never cross paths with them again. So why risk holding onto grudges and then regretting it when I eventually realize the value of forgiveness and the fleeting nature of our interactions?

"But not every time are you at fault and need to apologize, Grandpa!" I said in a lower tone.

"That's true," he replied. "Forgiveness and apologies aren't always about who is at fault but about how things are said. Even if someone is wrong, there are better ways to address it. We can convey our message and emotions in ways that don't escalate the situation but rather promote understanding and resolution."

"But not every time do I have to forgive. Sometimes, a tit for tat is necessary. The problem is when everyone believes it should be the case every single time."

I remember a fight I had with a friend during my school days. We were both in seventh grade. What started as a funny banter turned into a series of insults, and my friend crossed the line by making a personal comment. I couldn't take it. I didn't fight back or say anything in return; I was just quietly disappointed in him for taking things too far. I remained silent.

He realized his mistake after a few hours and came to apologize, but I didn't accept it. He turned away and left. The next day at school, he approached me as if he was about to start a conversation, but I didn't encourage him and walked away. This continued for a few days until he eventually gave up, realizing he couldn't get through to me. I, too, didn't care to go and talk to him. I always believed I shouldn't be the one to make the first move.

After a few months, and having missed out on memories and opportunities at school, we moved to eighth grade. He was placed in a different class, and we never had the chance to talk again.

As time passed and I spent more time with my group of friends, I began to recall the best memories we shared and realized how a single conversation led me to lose a friend forever. He might have been wrong, but I could have forgiven him, if not immediately, then eventually, or at the very least when he apologized. Instead, my ego took over. Looking back, the mistake now seems minor. It's natural to have discussions and debates among friends, especially those who are close to you. Those closest to you know you well and can make comments that push the limits. This doesn't necessarily make them right, but it's important to see it from a different perspective. When you're close to someone and they know everything about you, it's vital to focus on the positives. If it was indeed a mistake, address it and forgive.

Don't be so concerned with appearing strong by refusing to forgive; sometimes, true strength lies in letting go. To forgive is to show strength; to withhold forgiveness is to display weakness.

Remember, if you don't forgive someone, it doesn't change what has already happened. Unless someone has committed a crime or their actions were seriously harmful, disruptive, or emotionally and physically damaging, you have every right to choose not to forgive.

For example, if someone kidnapped your daughter and the police questioned you about the culprits, choosing not to forgive them and advocating for their imprisonment is entirely justified. I'm not referring to such grave situations. What I'm talking about are the incidents where someone may have wronged you, or you feel they did, often because you were too strict in understanding their perspective or because your reaction was more intense than necessary.

If my friend made personal comments about me, I should have expressed my anger or warned him not to do it again, rather than holding onto the grudge forever. If my sister liked someone whom I didn't think was right and he and I had a disagreement over it, I should have forgiven them for the sake of their happiness, rather than trying to impose my own perceptions about him on my sister.

"Did that grandma marry someone you didn't like?" I asked, referring to my grandpa's sister.

"Yes, she did," he replied. "He was a businessman. I didn't like the idea of her not having a steady income in those days and was worried about her financial security. I vehemently opposed their marriage and told her I wouldn't forgive her if she went through with it."

The discussions between us went on for a long time as we both tried to convince each other. Neither of us could agree on the other's point of view, and we ended up merely debating why our own perspectives were correct.

After a few months of trying, she gave up on convincing me and went ahead with the marriage. I was furious and taken aback. I told myself that despite all the care and love I had for my sister, she failed to understand my concerns for her. Her safety was my only concern, and she disregarded it to follow her own decision.

I decided that I would never forgive her for what she did and promised myself that I would never allow her to see me or my family again. She tried to communicate with me several times, but I ignored her calls. She also attempted to meet my mother, and initially, I refused to let her see her. However, eventually, my mother couldn't resist for too long and began staying in touch with her, helping her whenever needed.

After a few years, I learned that her family was moving to a different city for business, and my mother urged me to set aside my anger and talk to her before they left. Despite her insistence, I barely cared and remained steadfast in my unforgiving stance.

Later, I found out from my mother that their business had been successful and that they had become a wealthy and prominent family in town, with their business expanding across multiple states.

When my mother fell sick, my sister and her husband came to visit. Before they could speak to my mother, they asked for my forgiveness. After years of holding onto my ego and viewing life through a narrow lens, I finally decided to forgive her.

After I spoke with her and her husband, I was convinced that she had made the right decision. Seeing her children thriving and witnessing the success of her family made me realize how misguided I had been to believe that my perception was the only valid perspective. I had never really listened to my sister, who had tried to explain that they might succeed once their business picked up. I was swayed only by the situations and my own narrow view from those earlier times, never truly considering her viewpoint. I was proven wrong, and despite being in the wrong, it was I who eventually forgave. Recognizing the mistake, I had made, I asked for their forgiveness in return.

I realized that if I had forgiven them earlier, I could have been part of their family's growth and happiness sooner. I would have been happier myself and could have contributed to their happiness as well.

I realized that forgiving would improve the future, while holding onto resentment wouldn't change the past or affect what's to come.

When I visited an island in the west, I came across a village called Dunridge. The people there had a unique culture and a distinct way of perceiving things compared to the majority of the world. In this village, there is an elected head who manages the basic infrastructure and necessities using government funds. Unlike typical government operations, however, the village operates largely based on the head's directives and guidance. Despite this, the head genuinely strives for the betterment of the community and makes decisions with the welfare of the villagers in mind.

Whenever someone in the village faced a problem, they would turn to the head for guidance. He would even address personal issues, such as family disputes. The judgments and resolutions were delivered under a grand oak tree situated at the center of the village, in the presence of the village council and the community.

Every Friday, the cases brought forward were discussed in the village's central gathering, much like court proceedings. The council and the head had established a system where each person in the village was given three forgiveness tokens. This meant that each individual could use these tokens to be forgiven for up to three mistakes committed by others in the village. However, there were specific guidelines on the types of mistakes that could be forgiven, and the consent of the victim was also considered in the process for some cases.

While exploring the village's traditions and speaking with the locals to understand their way of life, I heard an announcement that a judgment would take place under the oak tree in thirty minutes, and the village was required to attend. Seeing it as an opportunity to observe their judicial process, I asked an elderly man if I could accompany him to the judgment. He agreed but instructed me to remain silent and simply observe. I agreed and followed him to the gathering.

The villagers were gathered in groups, discussing the events and speculating on how the head would handle the case. I asked the old man if he knew what the case was about. He replied that a school kid had been killed by a teenager, and the child's family had brought the matter to the head for a fair judgment.

I was shocked by the news and asked why a teenager would kill a school kid and who he was. The old man replied, "The teenager is the son of one of the council members. He has been reckless throughout his life and this isn't his first appearance at a judgment. However, he has already used his two forgiveness tokens for theft and an accident. This is his last forgiveness token."

I was intrigued and curious about how the head would handle such a serious situation. When the head arrived, he had a brief discussion with the council and then asked both parties to present their sides of the story. After hearing from both sides, the head requested some time to review the judgment book of guidelines. He spent several minutes quietly examining the book, turning the pages back and forth, before returning to the council for further discussion.

I was as curious as the other villagers to see what the head would decide. After some time, the head addressed the crowd and said, "He can't be spared this time. After carefully reviewing the guidelines, the council has determined that the forgiveness pass cannot be used for a murder, especially of a child. The accused will be sentenced to life in prison. Since he is nineteen, he will be considered a young adult and will face a lifetime imprisonment."

Upon hearing the judgment, the teenager's parents began weeping uncontrollably, knowing they would lose their son to a lifetime in prison. The mother of the murdered child was also crying deeply over her loss and looked at the teenager's mother, who was clinging to her son and sobbing. The teenager, witnessing the grief around him, began to reflect on the gravity of his actions and realized the immense mistake he had made.

The mother of the murdered child approached the teenager and asked why he had killed her son. Through tears, he replied, "I never thought he would die. We had an argument, and in the heat of the moment, I pushed him hard to the ground. He struck his head on the hard rock. I always saw him as a younger brother, and I'm truly sorry."

The mother of the murdered child, tearful, approached the head and had a brief discussion with the council. The council members listened intently, and the crowd became eager to learn what was unfolding.

After some time, the head and council addressed the crowd once more. "The child's mother has requested that the forgiveness pass be considered valid for the accused. According to the guidelines, despite the severity of the crime, if the victim or someone directly related to the victim consents, the pass can still be considered valid."

The mother of the murdered child then spoke, saying, "I have lost my child forever, and he will never return, no matter what. I understand the pain of losing a child, and it's a feeling I will carry for the rest of my life. I would do anything to have him back. I don't want another mother to experience this same agony, so I am choosing to forgive this young man. However, to ensure he understands the gravity of his actions, I believe he should be sentenced to three years in prison. This time will allow him to reflect on his wrongdoing and experience guilt, providing an opportunity for change."

The council, the head, and the teenager's family all agreed to this resolution.

As the crowd slowly dispersed, the old man and I walked away from the oak tree. I had countless questions and started asking him:

Q: What's the purpose of the three passes of forgiveness? I've never heard of anything like this before.

A: The head believes that by forgiving someone, you give them an opportunity for genuine reflection. Sometimes, holding onto unforgiveness can lead to revenge and escalate conflicts, turning them into unending feuds. I once borrowed money from a friend and couldn't repay it. According to the guidelines, I was allowed to use my first forgiveness pass. Initially, I was relieved, thinking I'd never have to repay my friend. But the guilt weighed on me, and when my friend fell gravely ill, I couldn't bear it any longer. I returned the money and helped with his treatment. I've often wondered if I hadn't been excused, I might have sought more opportunities to avoid repaying. This approach might not work for everyone, and times are changing. Still, we believe in its effectiveness here. After all, it's only three chances.

Q: I don't think people are inherently good enough to change simply because they are forgiven. It doesn't make sense to me.

A: The intention behind the forgiveness passes is to build a communal sense of accountability and growth. This village is isolated, with limited external influence, so the forgiveness system is meant to work in a controlled environment where its principles can be most effective. While it's true that not everyone might change, the idea is to encourage goodness and self-reflection.

Consider this: there were two men who were enemies throughout their lives. When one was on his deathbed, he said to the other, "I'm sorry! Forgive me for everything I did to you." He then passed away. The survivor lived with the memory of that moment, haunted by the forgiveness he received. Technically, he won the conflict; he outlived his adversary. But the forgiveness left him with no chance to seek revenge or continue the feud. It's not about life or death as a victory, but rather about the deeper impact of forgiveness. In this sense, the one who forgave achieved a form of triumph over bitterness and conflict.

Q: But isn't it unfair not to punish the teenager who killed an innocent child? How could his mother forgive so easily?

A: Even if she hadn't forgiven him, her child wouldn't come back. It was a grave mistake, possibly the biggest mistake of the teenager's life. While he should be punished, sending him away for life would not undo the past. In fact, it would only create more suffering, two grieving mothers instead of one. The idea is to avoid making the situation worse than it already is. The forgiveness pass provides a chance for the teenager to reflect and potentially change, rather than perpetuating a cycle of suffering and vengeance.

Q: What if someone tries to exploit these passes, like taking advantage of the goodwill of people who have unlimited forgiveness to offer?

A: The pass doesn't guarantee automatic forgiveness; it merely encourages forgiveness as a primary option. There are various other options and guidelines in place. The head evaluates each situation carefully, considering the nature of the mistake or crime before deciding whether to grant forgiveness. It's essential to be discerning about who deserves forgiveness. Kindness should not be confused with ignorance. The law of nature does not always spare those who exploit leniency or attempt to game the system.

Q: Who came up with these passes? Was it the Head?

A: No, it was the Head's grandfather. In their time, people were so quick to anger those trivial issues, like a lingering stare, a delayed response, or a loud call could escalate into fights. The concept of forgiveness was almost nonexistent; mistakes were often met with further retaliation. To encourage patience and kindness, he introduced these forgiveness passes. Over time, they helped people learn to pause and reflect rather than seek immediate revenge. The idea was that if you had to wait and think before reacting, you'd often realize the futility of continuing a conflict. For example, if someone accidentally slapped you and you had to wait two hours, staring at the person without reacting, you might find yourself more inclined to move on rather than prolong the confrontation. This approach gradually reduced anger and conflict, making people more patient and less prone to violence.

Q: I never realized forgiveness could have such an impact on people. What do you think about it?

A: As much as your mind might resist the idea of forgiveness, that resistance often reflects your reluctance to let go. Sometimes, you have to release the burdens that weigh you down, much like shedding excess weight when climbing a mountain. Forgiving and letting go of those who have wronged you can lift that weight, allowing you to climb higher and progress further. The more you release those grudges, the more you can elevate yourself, both emotionally and spiritually.

Forgiveness is about letting go of past wrongs and the people who have hurt you. The less weight you carry, the lighter you feel, and the higher you can climb.

That visit to the village, learning about their principles of forgiveness, and my conversation with the old man had a profound impact on me. It helped me embrace and practice forgiveness in my own life. There are many such inspiring examples around the world, and we should strive to learn from them.

I remember reading about Nelson Mandela's remarkable journey of forgiveness. His story is profoundly tangled with his transition from twenty-seven years of imprisonment to becoming South Africa's first Black president and guiding the nation through a critical process of resolution.

Mandela was imprisoned for his role in fighting apartheid, a brutal system of racial segregation and oppression in South Africa. Despite enduring harsh conditions and profound injustices, Mandela's dedication to his cause and his vision for a democratic South Africa remained unwavering.

Upon his release in 1990, Mandela faced the monumental task of guiding South Africa through a transition from apartheid to democracy. Instead of seeking retribution against those who had oppressed him and his people, Mandela chose a path of forgiveness and reconciliation. This approach was pivotal in preventing a civil war and promoting a peaceful transition.

Mandela's personal acts of forgiveness were also symbolic and impactful. One notable instance was his decision to invite his former jailer to his inauguration as president. By extending this gesture, Mandela demonstrated that he was willing to look beyond past grievances and work towards unity.

Mandela's approach to forgiveness was not about forgetting the injustices or condoning them, but rather about creating a foundation for a new, inclusive South Africa.

Nelson Mandela forgave those who had imprisoned him for twenty-seven years, choosing not to seek revenge. His path was to move forward, not backward. He understood that forgiveness allowed him to release the burden of resentment, enabling him to focus on the future and the work ahead.

Nowadays, people often struggle to spare even twenty-seven seconds for others. Our impatience has become so extreme that even minor delays can trigger our frustration. We see it in everyday scenarios: people fighting in queues because someone took too long, or drivers honking furiously if another car doesn't move the instant the light turns green. If we can't manage to be patient with these small inconveniences, how can we possibly find it within ourselves to forgive someone for more significant wrongs?

Forgiveness is not just an isolated emotion; it's deeply connected to the causes behind it. Many disputes arise from our own impatience. To truly forgive someone, you must practice patience. Nelson Mandela, despite spending twenty-seven years in prison, was able to forgive and move forward because he cultivated an immense sense of patience.

There are many events that highlight the power of forgiveness. For example, after the tragic shooting at an Amish schoolhouse in Pennsylvania, where a gunman took ten young girls hostage and killed five before ending his own life, the Amish community, known for their deep commitment to forgiveness, publicly forgave the shooter. They even reached out to his family, offering support and financial assistance.

Similarly, in the case of Jean and her son Joshua, who were involved in a severe accident caused by a drunk driver, Jean chose to forgive the driver despite the extensive legal process and the serious injuries her son sustained. She advocated for leniency, focusing on understanding and healing rather than seeking retribution. These stories underscore how forgiveness can bring about profound healing and reconciliation, even in the face of immense suffering.

As I recall such incidents, I remember a property dispute involving my friend where a lack of forgiveness led to chaos within the family.

My friend's father bought three acres of land on the outskirts of the city at a very low price. He had a younger brother, and over time, the city developed into a major hub with an airport linking multiple cities by air and road. A tech multinational company established itself near the land, causing its value to quadruple. At the time of purchase, my friend's father needed additional financial support and turned to his brother for help. However, his brother declined, dismissing the investment as a waste of money given the land's distant location from the city.

Despite his brother's skepticism, my friend's father went ahead with the purchase, anticipating the land's future value surge. He secured additional funds from the bank and repaid them over the following years. When the land's value eventually skyrocketed, his brother regretted not being involved in the investment and felt unhappy about missing out on the opportunity.

He approached his elder brother, asking for a share of the land by offering to pay for the initial investment. This request, which seemed unreasonable given the circumstances, was declined by my friend's father. He refused to sell the land or make his brother a partner.

Furiously, the younger brother took drastic action to damage the land owned by his elder brother. He dug holes and cut down trees across the entire three acres just before it was set to be sold. The elder brother was bewildered by this destructive act. In reflection, he realized that forgiving his younger brother and selling the land, despite the damage, would have been the wiser choice, as the land's value would not have decreased significantly without the trees.

However, he chose not to forgive and felt that his younger brother's reaction was unacceptable. Although his frustration was understandable, he could have either warned him or forgiven him instead of escalating the situation further.

The elder brother responded by escalating the conflict further. He cut down the trees, destroyed the garden, and damaged the newly built pool and garage at his younger brother's house. The cycle of retaliation continued, with both brothers' reactions growing increasingly intense.

What began as a petty dispute between the brothers eventually escalated into a tragic and violent confrontation. The conflict turned deadly when my friend's father was brutally attacked and killed by his younger brother at his own home. Enraged by the murder, my friend, before the police could intervene, incited others to take vengeance on his uncle, the man who had killed his father.

The cycle of violence continued as the younger brother's son attacked my friend in retaliation for the death of his father. My friend, in turn, retaliated against him. After a series of violent confrontations, both ended up in prison. Tragically, my friend died there due to a severe illness he contracted while imprisoned.

A simple act of forgiveness could have prevented the entire chain of vengeful actions that ensued, saving both parties significant loss of time, life, and energy.

The next time you feel impatience rising, take a deep breath and step away from the situation. Impatience often leads to impulsive decisions and hasty reactions, which can have lasting consequences.

That doesn't mean you should avoid tough situations altogether. It's just as important to be courageous as it is to be a smart decision-maker. Facing challenges with a clear mind allows you to handle them effectively and wisely.

Sometimes, it's crucial to conserve your energy, force, and aura for things that truly matter. Walking away from a fight without escalating it isn't an act of cowardice; rather, it's a brave choice that might not feel gratifying in the moment but will prevent future regret.

I was once dragged into a street fight over a minor argument with a stranger who confronted me for staring at him in the supermarket, even though I was simply looking around for the parking exit.

I had the courage to tell him to calm down and walk away, explaining that his assumptions were mistaken. But instead of letting it go, I chose to push him back when he shoved me. The situation escalated quickly, turning into a full-blown street fight. Despite ending up with a torn shirt and a broken nose, I declared myself the winner. Still, the victory didn't bring me any satisfaction.

I didn't look too great either after the fight. People around me regarded me with disdain, and I was summoned to the police station because the supermarket owner had filed a complaint against both of us. It ended up costing me money, time, and energy, and left me with a deep sense of regret.

If I had only forgiven that fool for his ignorance masked as arrogance, I would have had one less regret. Always remember to forgive others for their behavior, understanding that something within them might be driving their actions. Forgiving doesn't make you weak; it shows strength and wisdom. You don't need to prove your courage to everyone you encounter. Adopting a defensive attitude can make the world seem like it's against you.

Consider this exercise: while driving through busy city streets, try maintaining a serious expression. If someone honks at you, glare back; if another driver tries to overtake you, scowl. Keep this stern demeanor even when stopped at traffic signals or when someone drives recklessly near you. By the end of your drive, you might feel like everyone is impatient and aggressive.

This exercise illustrates how our own attitude and reactions can shape our perception of the world around us. If we approach situations with anger or defensiveness, we're more likely to encounter similar responses from others, reinforcing our negative feelings. However, if we approach with patience and understanding, we might find the interactions to be more positive and less confrontational.

Now, try the opposite approach: drive with a calm, friendly demeanor. Smile and show patience. If someone tries to overtake you, let them pass and smile. If someone honks excessively, yield and smile. If a driver nearly collides with you, stop and gently smile, asking if everything is okay.

By adopting this approach, you might find that the atmosphere of your drive becomes more relaxed and positive. People often respond to our demeanor and actions, so your kindness and calmness can help diffuse potential conflicts and adopt a more harmonious environment. You'll likely notice that others are more inclined to reciprocate your positive behavior, making the entire experience less stressful and more pleasant.

By forgiving others' mistakes on the road, you not only avoid unnecessary conflict but also encourage a more positive interaction. Often, your calmness will prompt others to reflect on their behavior, making them more likely to respond kindly and reducing the likelihood of future road rage.

Forgiveness surpasses revenge; it allows you to win without engaging in conflict. When you forgive someone, you elevate yourself beyond their actions and become a better person in the process. That, in itself, is a victory.

I wish I travelled more

I've always wanted to see the Northern Lights and had once planned a trip to Norway to do just that, but I couldn't make it for various reasons. My dedication to work and responsibilities often meant I settled for less when it came to traveling. Looking back, I realize that traveling more could have greatly expanded my perspective. I regret not seizing more opportunities to explore and wish I had ventured out more often.

"Does traveling really make a difference? Is it something to regret?" I asked, surprised.

"It does," my grandpa replied. "While you don't have to visit every country or island on the planet, I highly recommend traveling as much as you can. Exploring different places can have a profound impact on your life, broadening your perspective in ways you might not expect."

We are mere specks in the vast expanse of this infinite universe. Among billions of galaxies and countless stars, our planet orbits a single star, the Sun, for nearly four billion years. Despite the enormity of space, there are only around 200 countries on our small planet, and every person, whether known or unknown, born or deceased, has called this tiny world their home.

You might not know anyone who isn't from this planet, yet we have an astonishing array of cultural aspects, languages, currencies, governments, and more. There are countless divisions among us. Sometimes I wonder who truly owns this planet. The answer is nobody. Yet, we find ourselves bound by borders and restrictions, which puzzlingly highlights the planet's beauty. Its diversity, in all its forms, is what makes the planet, our home so uniquely captivating. Would you not regret exploring this tiny home as much as possible?

Do you realize that our bodies are essentially chemical factories? They operate through a complex interplay of chemical emissions and secretions, and our emotions are closely tied to these chemical processes. Traveling influences many of these hormones and chemicals, often triggering positive changes in how we feel and experience the world.

Hormone	How Travel Affects Release
Dopamine	New experiences and exploration can boost dopamine levels.
Serotonin	Exposure to new environments and cultures can enhance serotonin production.
Oxytocin	Traveling with others nurtures bonding and can increase oxytocin levels.
Endorphins	Engaging in activities like hiking or adventure sports during travel can release endorphins.
Cortisol	A change of scenery can help reduce chronic stress, leading to healthier cortisol levels.
Adrenaline	Adventure and excitement in travel can stimulate adrenaline

	production.

One of my friends was quite wealthy, with enough money to support himself and his family for several years even if he stopped earning. Yet, he always felt as though he didn't have enough and was never truly satisfied. He constantly experienced a sense of loss and never felt abundant. In search of clarity, he consulted a sage, who advised him to visit Varanasi in India and seek the blessings of the divine. The sage promised that this pilgrimage would help him feel a sense of abundance and relief.

Following the sage's advice, he traveled alone to Varanasi for a week. He booked a lavish hotel by the riverbank, where he had a view of the river Ganges from his window. On his first morning in the city, he woke up before sunrise and began his walk through the narrow, winding streets towards the riverbank. Along the way, he encountered many sages clad in simple saffron cloths, barely covering their upper bodies.

It was winter, and despite wearing his branded leather Armani jacket, my friend found the cold unbearable, walking with his hands stuffed in his pockets. He was astonished to see several sages emerging from the river after taking a dip in the frigid water. Remarkably, they didn't even dry off with towels. They simply tied their hair in a bun, wrapped their saffron cloths around themselves, and began walking with a steady pace, chanting "Om Namah Shivaya."

Curious, my friend stopped one of the sages and asked, "Saint, don't you feel cold?" The sage replied, "I do, but I don't let it bother me. My focus isn't on the cold but on the devotion within me. I'm heading to the temple to offer my prayers. This cold won't stop or disturb me." With that, the sage continued his brisk walk, undeterred by the winter chill.

My friend was astonished. It was 5:45 AM, and at that hour, he would usually be asleep in a heated room, lying on a teak cot with imported bedding, in a spacious bedroom with wooden floors, yet he would still wake up feeling dissatisfied and wanting more.

This realization struck him deeply, and he continued his journey towards enlightenment.

As he approached the temple, he saw a few women setting up their small stalls. Their children were strapped to their backs in cloth pouches. These women were arranging garlands and other offerings for visitors to purchase for their prayers.

He approached one of the women and asked, "Don't you feel tired waking up so early to set up your shop with your child sleeping on your back?"

She responded, "Yes, I do feel tired. But this is just how it is. If I don't wake up and set up my stall, the pilgrims will buy from other shops that are open. If that happens, I'll lose out on sales, and I won't be able to feed my children that day."

My friend asked her, "Do you ever feel unlucky because of this life you lead?" He wanted to know if she felt anything similar to his own sense of dissatisfaction.

She replied, "I'm able to set up this shop by myself. If God blesses me, I'll make profits during the busy seasons and save them for the quieter days. Look at Ram," she said, pointing to a middle-aged man across from her who was struggling to untie a rope. "He had an accident and lost his arm. Poor He is still managing his shop on his own while caring for his ailing mother. I have a perfectly functioning body and can handle everything myself. Why should I consider myself unlucky?"

My friend smiled with a pang of guilt and gave her some cash. He realized how he had failed to appreciate what he already had, focusing instead on what he lacked. He understood that the life he was living was a dream for someone else and that he had not been grateful for it. As he walked away, tears filled his eyes, marking a profound moment of realization and gratitude.

His entire week in Varanasi was a journey of realization and enlightenment. By the time he returned home, he was a changed man. His perspective on life had shifted profoundly, and the excitement with which he recounted his experiences to me and our friends made it clear that the trip had been truly transformative.

It wasn't that he hadn't encountered similar people in his own city, he had. But he had never taken the time to notice, interact with, or reflect on them.

Sometimes, the places we visit compel us to see things differently, offering us a new lens through which to learn and grow.

Once, my colleagues and I planned a trip to a mountain range, and we were all eagerly looking forward to it. However, your grandmother didn't want me to go because her father was visiting us, and she felt it would be inconsiderate for me to leave during that time. We had an argument, and I ended up leaving for the trip a day early. I stayed with one of my friends who was also part of the trip. I was feeling incredibly frustrated and exhausted from work, things going wrong at home, and financial losses. I really needed that vacation to recharge and escape from it all.

If I hadn't made the decision to go on that trip, I would likely be regretting more about not travelling enough. It turned out to be one of my most memorable experiences. We were a group of eight friends setting out to explore the stunning mountain ranges in the North.

As we reached our destination, I was captivated by the breathtaking scenery: towering mountains, river valleys, and stunning flower gardens. Rolling down the window of our vehicle, I felt the refreshing breeze rush past my face. The fragrance of flowers filled the air, and sunlight gently filtered through the vehicle. The sounds of chirping birds, the flowing water, and the cool breeze left me mesmerized. I was completely immersed in the beauty around me, momentarily losing myself in the mountain ranges and forgetting all my problems. While I knew this sense of peace wouldn't last forever, I realized that, for now, it was enough.

When you travel, you carry your luggage with you. Fortunately, your sorrows and griefs won't fit inside it.

As we enjoyed our time at the camp, sitting around the campfire and sharing laughter and stories, I realized how much the environment can influence our experiences. Back home, whether at our houses, offices, or gatherings, the conversations often revolved around sorrows, problems, debts, and complaints. It wasn't that we didn't have joyous stories to share, but we were rarely in the right environment to bring them out.

Sometimes, when you feel exhausted, tired, or stuck in life, it might not be just a mental issue, it could also be physical surroundings. If you're confined to the same place, the same routines, and unchanging environments, how can you expect your mental patterns to shift? Changing your surroundings can often be the key to refreshing your perspective and breaking free from stagnation.

When you travel the same routes, work in the same office, and lie in the same bed day every day, it's easy to feel stuck and depressed. Sometimes, it's not just the bed that needs changing, but its location. Try spending a few days somewhere new, away from your usual environment, and you'll likely find yourself feeling revitalized and refreshed.

Let me tell you another regretful story. There was a time when one of my close friends moved to a different city for his studies. He was a dear friend, and we used to hang out together most days of the month. After he relocated, he found a small apartment to rent and lived there alone. He had a few personal issues he often discussed, and I would reassure him that things would eventually work out and that there was no need to worry.

As he settled into his new city, it took him some time to adjust to the unfamiliar surroundings and people. He spent his days studying and his evenings alone, lost in his thoughts. He called me a few times, expressing how lonely he felt and asking me to visit him. I always hesitated, partly due to the hassle of traveling to a remote location, crossing borders, and changing multiple vehicles. I kept promising him that I would visit soon, but I never did. It wasn't that I didn't want to see him, he was a dear friend, but sometimes, the effort of traveling can seem daunting. While not all travel is enjoyable, it's important to remember that sometimes we travel not just for the journey, but merely for the destination, to reach somewhere.

Despite the importance of traveling to reach my friend, I was lazy and kept avoiding it. Even though he called me multiple times, he eventually realized that I wasn't coming. His loneliness and mounting problems grew overwhelming, and tragically, he decided to take his own life. Fortunately, he was quickly taken to the hospital when his door was unanswered for his neighbors.

I deeply regret not making the effort to visit him. I now understand that taking that one bus could have made a difference and possibly helped my friend to beat his depression and sadness. We both had a rift after that incident yet I talked to him once in a while after that to check how he was doing. I do regret it often.

If you pay close attention, you'll notice that this one planet is home to a vast array of cultures, languages, people, and traditions. Your feelings, perspectives, and reactions are often shaped by your environment. The way you speak, act, and think is largely a reflection of the social group you are part of. While not every aspect of your identity is influenced by this "herd," much of it is.

When you're removed from your familiar surroundings and placed in a different environment, you'll likely react and adapt in new ways. Even if your core perceptions remain unchanged, your responses to situations and people can shift significantly.

Imagine being suddenly relocated to a remote village in Russia, where you find yourself in a dilapidated house. Your only neighbors are an elderly Russian-speaking couple, and the nearest store is a ten-mile walk away through desolate, barren lands and abandoned radioactive zones. It's moderately cold, and you're expected to live alone. How would you react?

In such a situation, the harsh and isolating environment might prompt you to reassess your priorities and relationships. You might find yourself unexpectedly forming a close bond with the elderly couple, perhaps even befriending someone you once considered an enemy over there. The challenging circumstances and isolation would likely drive you to connect with those around you in ways you might not have imagined before, all because of the influence of your surroundings.

Next time you have a person with differences, a friend, or someone you like, consider traveling with them. The shared experience of a journey can often shift your perspectives and deepen your connection. By the end of the trip, you might find that your opinions have changed and that you've formed a stronger bond unless you're too persistent to adapt to change.

Imagine being suddenly placed in a vibrant, busy city in United Kingdom. The buildings are grand and towering, the streets are filled with flashy lights, and superfast cars zip by. People around you are impeccably dressed and exude appealing fragrances. The climate is mild, with an overcast sky hinting at a possible rain. As you navigate the city streets, you're enveloped in a sense of wonder, feeling as though you're stepping into a future world. Your senses are overwhelmed by the spectacle around you. Doesn't that experience sound exhilarating? Isn't it something you'd want to feel before you die?

Or imagine being in the midst of an Egyptian city, where you can see the colossal pyramids from a distance. The intricate sculptures, ancient carvings, and the preserved mummies captivate your senses. Picture yourself riding a camel across a deserted stretch of desert on your way back to the city, surrounded by the awe-inspiring relics of a bygone civilization. The experience would be steeped in history and wonder, offering a unique clue into the magnificence of ancient Egypt. Doesn't it sound amazing?

Or picture yourself in the middle of the Amazon rainforest, crossing a narrow river among the dense vegetation. The adventure is intense as you navigate the waters, with crocodiles prowling beneath the surface. The trees loom so close that they brush against your head when you stand up in your small boat. On the riverbanks, you catch sights of interesting animals, and the chirping of birds fills the air. The experience is both thrilling and immersive, offering a thoughtful connection with the wild beauty of the rainforest. Would you not want to experience such adventures?

Or find yourself in a speed train in Korea, enjoying lunch in an Indian restaurant, browsing a toy shop in Japan, or visiting a museum in Australia. Each experience is unique and enriching. Travel and explore as much as you can before it's too late.

The great thing about travel is that you always return home once it ends, but the memories stay with you forever. You'll cherish them for as long as you live.

In our neighborhood, there was an elderly couple who seemed to very much in love. Their children lived abroad and visited them only once a year. Now retired, the couple spent their days together in their home. The husband had a passion for gardening, and his home was decorated with numerous pots and a few saplings in the backyard. I would often see him joyfully watering his plants while singing retro songs.

The wife was a writer, penning articles for newspapers and books on culture and life lessons. While they were happy together, they often felt bored. At that time, I was in my forties. One day, I decided to invite myself over to their home, hoping to engage in conversation to ease their boredom and perhaps gain some insights on life from this experienced couple.

I knocked on their door one Sunday morning. The old man answered, looking a bit puzzled as if he hadn't been expecting anyone. I introduced myself as their neighbor and mentioned that I had come to say a quick 'Hello.'

He welcomed me with a warm smile and introduced me to his wife. She offered me cookies and a hot coffee, which were delicious. As we chatted, I gradually began asking about them, learning about their past work in the medical field and their children who were working in the States.

I asked the couple how they spent their time and invited them over for coffee. They graciously accepted, explaining that they had traveled extensively around the world since their marriage. Now, in their later years, they felt a need to stay home for a while. They mentioned that their next desired journey was to visit the largest temple in the world.

I was surprised to learn that the old couple had traveled all over the globe. Curious to know more, I asked them about their adventures. They shared that they had met and fallen in love at a hospital camp set up for flood victims. Their deep compassion for the sick led them to explore various medical treatments worldwide. They married against their families' wishes but remained happily together ever since.

Their exploration of medical sciences and passion for travel took them all over the globe during their early married years. They even spent their entire savings on these adventures, often returning home broke. Despite this, they always felt incredibly rich from the memories and experiences they had gathered along the way.

Sometimes, they would even borrow money from friends and family to fund their travels. After each trip, they would repay the loans by working double shifts at the hospital. Their ability to travel wasn't in question; it was their desire that drove them. Every new destination was approached with a minimalistic budget. They made it a point to engage with the locals, learning about the cultural, medical and traditional aspects of each place they visited.

They returned home not just with immense joy and pleasure, but with the pride of having embraced new places and cultures that few in their circle had experienced. Their travels and medical learning eventually led them to establish their own medical organization. This organization offered treatments for various diseases worldwide, leveraging their extensive knowledge and experience. They built a reputation for themselves, becoming a recognized name in their field for their innovative approaches to treatment and understanding of medical conditions.

As their financial situation improved, their lives became more seamless, allowing them to travel extensively. Their children went abroad for their higher studies, and the couple took the opportunity to explore numerous destinations. They visited nearly every corner of the globe, from European nations to the United States, Canada, Mexico, Colombia, Argentina, Cuba, Nigeria, Sudan, Dubai, Tokyo, New Zealand, and many more. They had truly seen it all.

As the husband shared their story, I went through the endless photo albums provided by his wife, each album filled with pictures from nearly every place they had visited.

By the end of the album, I felt as if I had taken a trip around the globe myself. I could appreciate how fulfilling it must have been for the couple to have traveled to so many places. Their experience was truly remarkable and rare. I was deeply impressed by their story and eager to continue the conversation about their incredible journey.

I asked them a few questions, and here's how they responded:

Q: Weren't you tired from all the extensive travel? How did you find excitement in long and sometimes boring journeys?

A:"Travel isn't just about the destination; it's about the journey as well. We view everything along the way as something exciting and new, a small restaurant, a grand tree, a straggling road, a windmill, and so on. There's always something to learn or see from a different perspective. Of course, there were times we felt bored and took naps. What else could we do? Ask time to speed up?" He laughed heartily as he answered.

Q: Did you ever feel you weren't ready to travel, whether financially, physically, or mentally?

A: "Readiness is never a perfect blend; it's just one emotion rising up while the rest try to catch up. When I visited Egypt, I sold my car to fund the trip. Financially, I wasn't prepared, but mentally, I was eager to see the Pyramids. It reminds me of my son, who wanted to lose weight and look great before visiting a beach for photos. I told him, 'It's not the pictures you take with a camera that matter, but the memories you capture with your eyes that last longer.' So, no, he wasn't physically ready, just like sometimes we weren't." He chuckled once more.

Q: Do you regret visiting any place?

A: "Yes, there was one instance when we visited an area in middle eastern world and lost our luggage, which contained most of our money. We had to hitch rides to get to the central part of town to withdraw more funds. But even that wasn't too bad. Aside from that, we have no regrets. People often think regrets come from visiting good and bad places, but that's not necessarily true. Our goal was never just to enjoy but to explore. Even what some might consider 'bad' places can be the most interesting during exploration."

Q: What do you say if someone tells you that you're just wasting time and money?

A:"Many people said that, especially when we borrowed money for our travels. We didn't see their opinions as constructive. Travel benefited us in numerous ways. The people we are today are largely shaped by our extensive experiences. If you ask anyone who knows us, they wouldn't have many negative things to say." He chuckled again.

Q: If I don't travel to explore or see new places, will I miss out on something?

A: "Everything. Life isn't just about waking up, traveling the same roads, reaching the same places, and returning home each day. If you live like that, you'll miss out on so much. Travel is a gateway to enlightenment. It stimulates both your physical and mental abilities. The more you challenge and move them, the better they perform. Life and death should be distinct, not one blending into the other. A robotic, routine existence is like a slow death. At the end of your life, if you haven't ventured out, you'll likely feel a deep emptiness. Don't let that happen."

After our conversation, I said goodbye and invited them for coffee. As I walked away, the words of the old couple continued to resonate with me. I reflected on the many opportunities I had to travel that I had missed.

There was a time when your grandmother and I won a five-day trip sponsored by a well-known beverage company. It was a prize for ten lucky customers who frequently bought their product. With so many relatives and friends visiting our home regularly, I always bought that beverage, never expecting anything in return.

When we were announced as winners, your grandmother was thrilled and immediately began planning what to pack and the clothes to bring. I was excited too! After spending so much on the beverages, it felt like a nice reward, and I didn't want to miss out on the opportunity.

As you know, it often seems like bad things happen just before good things. A week before the trip, I fell seriously ill. I was disappointed but not entirely regretful then, as I wasn't a huge fan of traveling anyway. I thought if I recovered in time, I'd still go on the trip.

I was partially recovered, and if I had fully committed and pushed myself to go on the trip, I might have made it. However, I chose not to. Instead of seizing the opportunity for the experiences it promised, I decided to rest in bed.

Your loving grandmother didn't want to go without me, and I deeply regret that decision now. In hindsight, I should have encouraged her to take the trip, which might have made me feel less regretful about missing out.

Reflecting on the old couple's experiences, I realized how I missed an opportunity to explore new places with your grandmother and create cherished memories. Instead, I ended up with a regret that can't be undone.

Sometimes, a straightforward 'No' can save time and energy. However, a hasty 'No' can lead to regrets later.

Mastering the art of when to say 'No' is a delicate balance worth achieving.

"Do you remember any times when you said 'No' to travel plans?" my grandpa asked me.

I replied, "A few times! Most of my friends do that too; they back out at the last minute."

Grandpa laughed, "Ha-ha! That's a common issue among friends from our ages, but try your best to visit places as much as you can. I understand that factors like finances, time, and the location matter, but you're smart enough to know if a trip is worth the memory. If it is, don't skip it."

As he said this, I remembered a beautiful trip I skipped because I wasn't feeling up to it and instead stayed in my cozy bed, watching Netflix. My friends posted pictures and shared their amazing memories after returning, and I felt a sense of regret. I promised myself that I'd make an effort to go on a few trips in the coming months and started listening to my grand pa more attentively.

"What's next, Grandpa?" I asked, my curiosity piqued.

He replied, "I'm feeling tired now. I'll rest for a bit. Please ask the nurse if she can arrange for us to meet again in the morning."

I realized it was getting late and that he had a surgery scheduled in two days "Okay, Grandpa! You get some rest. I'll see you tomorrow. Think about your other regrets and share your best memories with me," I said.

He smiled and said, "I remember my regrets very well. I need not recall them."

I nodded, wished him goodnight, and left the room, taking the elevator down to the ground floor.,

As I passed by, I noticed a nurse peeking in. I caught her eye and asked, "What are you looking at?"

She replied, "I was listening to your conversation from the beginning and couldn't leave until it was over. It seems like he's tired now, so I'll wait until tomorrow to hear the rest."

I smiled with pride and replied, "I guess so. Please take good care of him. He's not confident about making it through, but I know it's just his fear, like everyone else feels before a surgery."

"I will look after his medicines and food and will let you know if anything is needed," she said.

I thanked her and headed downstairs. As I drove home, I decided to take a longer route, reflecting on his insights about travel. I avoided the shorter path and took a U-turn, savoring the extra time to contemplate his words.

As I took the longer route home, avoiding the usual shortcut, I began to notice details I had never seen before. The familiar streets revealed hidden nooks and crannies, each with its own story to tell. I passed a small park where the homeless were sleeping on benches, and saw a couple of elderly people engaged in a game of chess under the street light beating their inability to sleep.

Along the way, I came across an old bookstore which was still open. I had never noticed despite passing by countless times. Intrigued, I stepped inside and was greeted by shelves stacked with books of all genres. As I browsed, a particular title caught my eye, a book on travel adventures around the world. I struck up a conversation with the bookstore owner, who turned out to be an avid traveler himself. He shared captivating stories of his journeys, igniting a newfound wanderlust within me.

Reflecting on the day as I finally arrived home, I realized that taking the longer route had not only exposed me to new sights and experiences but had also taught me the value of slowing down and appreciating the journey itself. By avoiding the shortcut, I had opened myself up to unexpected encounters and gained insights that enriched my perspective on travel and life.

After I read half of the book in one go, I slipped into a deep sleep. However, I woke up with an excitement to learn more stories from my grandpa and try to relate to my life experiences. While I was getting ready to meet him again, I also remembered it was his surgery day after tomorrow and I was anxious about how it would go. I tried to tell myself, everything will be alright and went to meet him at the hospital in the next morning. I reached his bed again and there he was resting with his eyes wide open as if they were searching for someone.

As soon as he saw me, his eyes sparkled a little and welcomed me. I sat beside him again and started to make a note of what he was saying again.

I wish I did not Overthink

Once, a mighty king commanded one of his ministers to cross the desert on a camel to find a treasure hidden at the beginning of a forest at the desert's end. As the minister rode his camel, he depleted all his water supplies halfway through the journey and soon became severely dehydrated. By the afternoon, the blazing sun was unbearable, but then he spotted a water pond in the distance. His eyes widened with hope, but as he approached, the pond seemed to recede further away, and eventually, it vanished altogether.

"Must be a water mirage," I interrupted my grandpa.

"Exactly," he replied. "A water mirage is an illusion that tricks you into thinking there's a pond in the hot desert, when in reality, it's just an optical effect caused by the refraction of light."

"That's what overthinking does too," He continued. "It creates thousands of mirages, making you feel like you've got countless problems or events that might trouble or please you. In reality, none of them exist, and they vanish once you move past that moment."

As you overthink, these mirages grow stronger. Yet, as time progresses and you approach these imagined events, they often don't happen or aren't as significant as you feared or hoped. Whether they are sad or joyous mirages, they ultimately lead you nowhere.

Overthinking creates imaginary scenarios in your head that never come to pass in reality. You end up living through these scenarios in your mind, feeling their effects as though they were real. What a foolish misuse of an extraordinary human ability.

I regret overthinking a few times in my life, and I wouldn't want you to make the same mistake. To understand overthinking, you first need to grasp the fundamentals of thinking. What is thinking? Why do we need to think? How can you know when and how much to think?

To think is essentially to process information. It's a mental activity, a cognitive process, that can happen with or without sensory input. Typically, thinking occurs internally and may also independently of external stimuli. It encompasses reasoning, concept formulation, judgment, problem-solving, and deliberation. It also involves ideas, memories, and imagination, collectively known as thoughts. In simpler terms, thinking is a mental process that happens within your mind and influences how you perceive and respond to various situations in your life. There's never a moment when you're not thinking; even when people say, "Don't think about it," you inevitably do.

To cease thinking would be to cease living. Thinking is a fundamental aspect of human existence. Each day, you engage in thought, and there will never be a day when you live without it.

When you act without thinking, you might find yourself in trouble. When you act with overthinking, you might still face difficulties. It's not just about thinking; it's about thinking correctly that truly matters.

What is overthinking?

Overthinking is when you excessively or compulsively analyze and dwell on a situation, problem, or thought. It involves repeatedly going over the same thoughts or scenarios, trying to anticipate every possible outcome or solution, or obsessing over minor details.

What happens when you overthink?

When you overthink, it can lead to increased stress, anxiety, and indecision. You may become trapped in a loop of mental deliberation that prevents you from taking action or moving forward. This often hampers effective problem-solving and can negatively impact your emotional well-being.

Let me tell you a funny story from when I was a kid. My mom gave me a coin and asked me to buy something from the grocery store. I took the coin and skipped through the narrow streets, singing and playing along the way. I tossed the coin into the air and tried to catch it as I walked. After a few successful catches, I threw the coin up so high that, when it came down, I couldn't grab it. It slipped from my hands, rolled across the road, and vanished into the busy street, hiding somewhere beyond an obstruction.

I was extremely worried and searched everywhere for the coin but couldn't find it. I looked beneath the cartons placed in front of a shop, checked behind them, and searched all around the area where I had lost it. But alas, the coin was nowhere to be found.

I thought I had lost the coin, and my mind started to overthink the situation. I imagined my mom would scold me severely for losing it. She might forbid me from playing with my friends in the evening, make me study for three hours without a break, and insist that I buy groceries every day from now on. My overthinking spun countless scenarios in my head, each one more daunting than the last.

"Like Dr. Strange?" I interrupted.

My grandpa looked at me with a hint of disappointment and said, "Yes, everyone who overthinks is a bit like Dr. Strange, but the difference is that Dr. Strange can also see possible positive outcomes."

I wasn't exactly like Dr. Strange. After imagining all the worst possible outcomes, I decided I couldn't go back home, my mother would surely scold me. So, I sat under a nearby tree and began to think about where the small coin could have rolled off to and disappeared in this space. I searched every-where, puzzled by how I could have missed it.

After a while, I saw my mom approaching where I was seat-ed. It dawned on me that more than an hour had passed since she sent me to buy something, and I hadn't returned home yet. She spotted me from a distance and started sprinting to-ward me. I braced myself, thinking that a slap on the face would be the least of my worries and that I'd regret my ac-tions.

As she got closer, I shouted, "Mom! I lost the coin. I searched everywhere and have no idea where it went. I'm sor-ry! I won't do it again."

My mom replied, "That's fine. But why didn't you come back home and tell me? I would have given you another coin. I was worried about where you went."

I was utterly shocked to hear that. While I didn't voice my thoughts, I told myself, "This is something I couldn't have foreseen. If I had lost the coin and just gone home to tell her, she would have given me another one without any punishment. All the scenarios and punishments I imagined were entirely created by me. I had thought up worse consequences for myself than anyone else could have, because only I knew my fears. So, not all the fears and scenarios we overthink in our heads actually come to pass."

But I simply said, "Okay, Mom," and went back home.

That's what overthinking looks like; it makes you suffer from things that aren't real. What do you call someone who suffers from something that doesn't exist? A lunatic.

Don't be one. I've been a lunatic at times myself. While it's not entirely possible to avoid overthinking, because recognizing when you've crossed the line from normal thinking can be difficult, especially since you might not even realize you've crossed it.

When to know if you're overthinking? Follow PPP.

I asked curiously, "What's that, Grandpa?"

He replied, "It stands for Pause-Pivot-Progress."

Pause: When you start sensing too many negative outcomes, take a moment to stop.

Pivot: Shift to another thought that's unrelated or force yourself to envision a positive outcome, even if you're not entirely confident in it. You have the skill to imagine a better scenario, use it.

Progress: By avoiding the negative thoughts and focusing on the forced positive or alternative thoughts, you'll be able to move forward with less fear and doubt in your current thought process.

For example, you might remember me from time to time, even after I'm gone. Your memory will start working and push you into a zone of thought. This might lead you to realize that I'm no longer here, and you might start missing me. Then, that thought zone can shift into an overthinking zone, where you either dwell on the same thought repeatedly or delve into negative emotions beyond the initial thought.

You might initially miss me and come to the painful realization that I'm not coming back, which can lead to feelings of sorrow and anxiety. You might then start replaying missed opportunities to talk to me, regrets about the time you didn't spend together, mistakes you made, and moments of anger towards me. This can spiral into remorse and lead to deeper feelings of depression, a sense of loss, and uncertainty about how to move forward or escape those feelings. This cycle can continue endlessly, with your overthinking causing negative emotions to evolve and intensify rapidly.

And, you'd find yourself lost in these thoughts, potentially losing a part of yourself, your time, and your energy, making your life feel miserable. But if you follow PPP: Pause, Pivot, Progress, you have a chance to avoid such a deep descent and mitigate the impact of overthinking.

When you realize you've missed me and start to enter the second zone of overthinking, dwelling on the fact that I'm gone forever, Pause. Don't plunge into revisiting bad memories, sad truths, or difficult moments. Instead, Pivot. Shift your focus away from those negative thoughts and force yourself to switch to something unrelated or positive. By making this a conscious decision, you increase the likelihood of successfully managing your overthinking and avoiding a downward spiral.

Deviate your thoughts toward things that evoke positive, pleasant emotions. Think about something you enjoy doing, your favorite place, a beloved TV show, or a fun time you had. Redirect your mind to those uplifting thoughts! You've already thought about me, missed me, and shown your love, even in my absence. That's enough gratitude. Now, let go of those thoughts and move on.

If shifting your thoughts is difficult, pivot towards positive feelings and memories you've shared with me. Reflect on the good times, the laughter, the fun, the places we visited, and the stories we shared, including these very final conversations. Transform the thoughts that might spiral into negative emotions into ones that evoke positivity and encouragement. Even if you find yourself overthinking, focusing on these positive memories will help you feel better. **Unfortunately, we often tend to dwell on what hurts us, rather than seeking solace in the good.**

"Let me tell you a story about you" my grandpa said.

"About me!", I exclaimed.

Yes, he continued, On the mountaintop where a holy temple stood, there was a monkey who lived there.

I realized his sarcasm and laughed within and continued to listen.

He continued, People would frequently trek up the mountain, navigating its toughest paths, to visit the temple and enjoy the breathtaking view of the mountain range from above.

This monkey was believed to be the guardian of the temple by the local people. The belief originated from someone in the local area and quickly spread through conversations, becoming widely discussed across the mountain range and among the pilgrims and tourists who visited.

The monkey was treated with special fruits and snacks, as it was regarded as a holy animal. Delighted by the offerings, the monkey didn't question why it was being treated so well. It simply accepted the generosity, believing there must be a reason for it. Initially, the monkey was curious and slightly apprehensive about the sudden abundance of food, pondering why it was receiving such special treatment. However, the allure of the delicious fruits quickly overshadowed its curiosity. It enjoyed the food and stopped questioning the reason behind it.

Meanwhile, the other monkeys in the troop living below the mountain had no knowledge of the temple and wondered where the holy monkey obtained such clean and tasty fruits.

One day, all the monkeys gathered to discuss the source of the holy monkey's food.

One of the monkeys suggested, "This monkey might have an unlimited reserve of food hidden somewhere in the village down the mountain."

Another monkey chimed in, "Perhaps the monkey has received superpowers from the old monkey who meditates in the caves. It might be able to conjure fruits from thin air with such powers."

As the discussions continued, one of the monkeys suddenly interrupted, "Enough! Let's follow him tomorrow and uncover his secret source."

The other monkeys agreed, eager to find out the truth.

The next day, the monkeys decided to follow the holy monkey. As it left its den, the holy monkey climbed a small rock, leaped across thirteen trees, swung from branches, took a dip in the flowing river, swam across the area, and finally climbed hundreds of broken stairs to reach the back of the temple at the mountaintop.

The monkeys who followed were shocked to discover this challenging path. Five monkeys had embarked on the journey to track the holy monkey.

As the holy monkey swung from a tree branch, one of the followers examined the branch and remarked, "That looks so weak, it might break any moment. I'm sure if I try to hold on, it will snap, and I'll fall and break my teeth. I don't care where that monkey gets its fruits from; I'm going back home."

The two monkeys who watched the holy monkey swim across the river said, "The river flows so fast. That monkey must be used to swimming here all the time. We would definitely get swept away and drowned. It looks too deep." Both decided to return home.

Among the remaining two monkeys, one said to the other, "Look at those old, abandoned stairs the monkey is using. This path is unlike anything we've ever taken. It's a wrecked place, and I'm sure the monkey is leading us somewhere dangerous to push us off the edge. I think I'll head back home too."

The last monkey remaining followed the holy monkey all the way to the mountaintop temple. It was astonished to see the pilgrims and tourists at the top of the mountain. However, it chose not to intrude, so it stayed at the edge of the wall it had climbed, observing the holy monkey from a distance.

The holy monkey entered the temple confidently, seemingly unaffected by the presence of people around. It settled into its favorite spot right below the new stairs at the front side of the mountain.

The pilgrims who had climbed the mountain through the rugged paths marveled at the holy monkey's presence. They offered fruits and snacks, as they believed it was a sacred guardian of the temple. The monkey, content and familiar with this routine, accepted the offerings with gratitude.

The pilgrims who climbed the mountain via those stairs passed by the holy monkey, bowing their heads in respect and offering bananas, apples, papayas, and other fruits and food items. The holy monkey took whatever it liked and allowed the rest to be placed in front of it. It ate the fruits slowly, gazing at the sky, never disrupting the tourists or questioning their actions. The monkey simply lived in the moment, content and at peace.

An old man, seeing the monkey on the edge of the mountain, assumed it was the holy monkey. He reached into his old bag, searching for a banana to offer. The old man, who had difficulty walking, used a stick to support himself as he made his way up the mountain.

He hurried to offer the banana to the monkey, who was watching the holy monkey from the edge of the mountain, while clutching a stick in his hand. The holy monkey, noticing the old man's approach, turned swiftly to see what he was carrying.

Startled, the monkey attempted to step back but, not realizing it was at the edge of the mountaintop, slipped and fell down onto the wrecked stairs far below. The fall resulted in severe injuries, and the monkey tragically died from the impact.

"Now, tell me, in what scenarios did the monkeys overthink?" my grandpa asked.

I: When they thought the monkey had an unlimited source of food?

Grandpa: Exactly! They overthought and conjured an outcome that was beyond their reach. They even imagined that the monkey had superpowers to obtain simple fruits, something they felt they couldn't achieve. Sometimes, overthinking becomes your own enemy, creating fears that hinder you. The truth was, the fruits were freely offered at the mountaintop, and they simply needed to go there to get them. Instead, their overthinking led them to believe they needed superpowers.

Similarly, when humans overthink, they often block their own path to success. Instead of taking simpler actions that could lead to results, they paralyze themselves with imagined disruptions and hurdles that don't actually exist.

I: The monkey that saw the branch and thought it was too weak to hold him?

Grandpa: Exactly! The branch might have been weak, but the monkey didn't give it a chance. It overthought that it would break, without even trying. If it had watched the other monkeys using the branch, it would have seen that it wasn't as weak as it imagined. Instead, it only considered the negative possibility of breaking its teeth.

Similarly, when you're paralyzed by overthinking, pivot to positive thoughts. If you can strongly believe in negative outcomes that haven't happened, why not also believe in positive outcomes that could? Look around to see that your fears might not be as real as they seem. If the monkey had observed the other monkeys swinging successfully, it would have gained the confidence to try itself.

When you're overthinking, take time to find examples where similar actions succeeded. There's always room to see that others have faced and overcome similar fears. If they could do it, so can you.

I: The two monkeys that assumed the river was fast and deep?

Grandpa: Yes. Those monkeys overthought that the river was both fast and deep. In reality, if the river were truly fast and dangerous, even the holy monkey wouldn't manage to cross it daily. The current was manageable, and with a little effort, they could have passed it. Moreover, rivers in mountainous regions are generally not very deep. The monkeys' assumptions were products of their overthinking, far removed from reality.

Similarly, when you find yourself overthinking and can't relate to examples, seek out the facts. Facts don't lie; they are objective truths. When faced with doubts, grounding yourself in factual information can help you see beyond the distortions of overthinking.

I: The monkey that didn't climb the stairs, assuming it would be pushed to its death?

Grandpa: Yes, that monkey did recognize that the stairs were old and wrecked, but it also saw a positive outcome, reaching the mountaintop despite the obstacles. However, it overthought the potential danger, imagining being pushed to death by the holy monkey.

Similarly, overthinking might not always happen before you start; it can occur during the process as well. When it does, remember to use PPP. Don't let overthinking stop you from moving forward smoothly.

I: The monkey that died falling off the edge, did it overthink? It seemed to handle all the tough paths without overthinking, right?

Grandpa: That's correct. The monkey successfully navigated all the challenging paths, swinging from branches, swimming across the river, and climbing the old steps. However, it overthought in that final moment. When it saw the old man approaching with a stick, it mistakenly believed the man was a threat rather than someone offering food. This fear led to the monkey slipping from the mountaintop and falling to its death.

I: But Grandpa, that monkey didn't really have time to think properly; it just thought wrong instead of overthinking.

Grandpa: Thinking wrong is indeed a subset of overthinking. When you assume something will go wrong before it even happens, that's part of overthinking. Yes, the monkey didn't have enough time to think clearly, but that doesn't excuse its mistaken assumptions.

This is true for humans as well. When we're under pressure or reacting from a place of fear, anxiety, or panic, we often end up thinking negatively or incorrectly. Why? Because we're forced to make decisions quickly, leaving little time for the right course of action.

"This is a skill that must be practiced, thinking quickly yet correctly, and thinking big in a short amount of time. It's a skill you improve with practice."

As soon as he finished his sentence, my grandpa reached for his medicines from the table beside him and slipped them from his hands.

I caught the medicines quickly, almost instinctively, and placed them back on the table.

My grandpa looked at me and said, "Just checking if you're capable of making the right decisions in a short time."

It was comforting to see him remain light-hearted and humorous despite his situation. I replied with a smile, "If you're quick, I'll be quick too."

He smiled and continued with his words of wisdom. "I had a friend who was a master of overthinking. If everyone on this planet were ranked from the most to the least prone to overthinking, he'd definitely be in the top hundred. And if I told him this, he'd start overthinking how he might not make it into the top hundred, wondering just how much more someone else could overthink compared to him."

He would overthink every scenario that he'd never actually lived in the present. His entire life seemed to pass by while he was fixated on the future or the past, neglecting the present. He spent his time worrying about what might happen or dwelling on what had already occurred. He was constantly preoccupied with how he could have changed the past or how grim the future might be for him.

Spending a few months with him led me to adopt his overthinking habits for a while, and letting them go proved challenging. To give you an idea of just how extravagantly he thought, I need to tell you about one particular day.

That day, we planned to catch a movie and agreed to meet at a specific point to take the bus. The day before, when I suggested catching the bus at 9:15 AM from the boarding point, he immediately began overthinking. He said, "If the bus is at 9:15 AM, I'll need to finish my breakfast by 8:30 AM and then walk quickly to the meeting point."

He continued, "Generally, I have my breakfast around 9:00 AM, so I'd need to ask my mother to cook it earlier. I'm not sure if she'll be able to, since she seemed sick today. Maybe I'll just have to eat out. That means I should start earlier than 8:00 AM. Oh no, I've got a pain in my right foot, so I won't be able to walk fast. I should walk slowly, which means I'd have to leave around 7:30 AM."

He went on, "I'm not sure if I'll be able to wake up by 6:30 AM tomorrow. I'm worried I'll miss my alarm, like I usually do on important days. I'll set three alarms back-to-back to make sure I wake up on time. But since I tend to stay up late, I'll need to go to bed early tonight."

"I'll head home soon so I can rest," he concluded.

His chain of overthinking continued, and I was left shocked, tired, and frustrated watching him spiral like that.

I said, "It's okay if you're a bit late; the bus will wait for 10 minutes at the stop. Your leg will be fine by tomorrow; it's just a minor wound. I just spoke to your mother, and she's fine too. If she can't cook for you, we can eat out after the movie or I can bring some snacks for you. Relax!"

He seemed relieved but still had a stream of thoughts running through his mind. Before he could say anything, I cut him off, saying, "Stop! Don't overthink it anymore. Just go home and take it easy."

The next day, I arrived at the meeting point at 9:20 AM and saw my overthinking friend already waiting there.

Before I could approach him, he shouted, "You're already five minutes late! The bus would have left in another five minutes and we both would have missed the movie. Why did it take you so long?"

I replied calmly, "I'm here right on time. I knew the bus would start at 9:20 AM. Even if we miss it, we can find alternative options. By the way, did any of your fears come true?"

"What fears?" he asked.

"The fears you had yesterday about making it here on time," I clarified.

He replied, "Well, I had the pain in my foot, so I took my medicine and went to bed early. I woke up before the alarm after having a sound sleep. My mom knew I was going to the movie and cooked the food early without me even asking. The medicine worked, my foot healed, and I was able to walk faster and get here on time."

"So, nothing that you overthought and feared yesterday actually happened, right?"

"Yeah," he admitted, "but they could have happened."

"If they had happened," I said, "it would make sense to feel bad about it. But you were anxious about something that didn't occur, something made up in your head due to overthinking. So, stop overthinking!"

As soon as I said that, my friend scratched his head, and I realized he hadn't understood a single word.

"I hope you understood what I said," my grandpa said to me.

I replied, "To live a situation in your head before it happens in reality is foolish."

A small correction: it's stupid if you're living a negative situation before it happens. You can imagine yourself in positive and uplifting situations there's no harm in that. But know your limits, because reality might differ from your imaginings.

Like my friend who worried about every possible issue before it even happened. He spent so much time and energy anticipating problems that never materialized. Those worries stole his present moment and, if they had come true, would have affected his future as well. Worrying about what hasn't happened can rob you of the present and weigh you down in the future.

So, if the worst things are set to happen tomorrow, cry tomorrow after they happen. Smile now, laugh now. Why live through the worst situations multiple times? Live them only once.

There lived an old man at the edge of the city, close to the ocean. When a tsunami alert was issued for the entire city, it was clear that his house would be swept away by the ocean the next day as the high tides hit.

He had every reason to cry for tomorrow, losing his beautifully built home and all his hard-earned money. But more than that, he had today to live. The previous night, he enjoyed his time watching TV in the living room, sitting on his favorite sofa and laughing out loud at a comedy show while eating snacks.

The next day, the high tides did hit his home, but they were not as severe as expected. His house remained mostly intact, with just a few scratches. He found that he had another day to be happy.

Even if his home had been washed away, he would have been only fifty percent sad over the two days, one for the tsunami alert and one for the destruction of his home, rather than spending both days crying and being completely miserable. By enjoying the present and not succumbing to unnecessary worry, he avoided losing two days to sorrow.

I know it's challenging, but that's exactly why you might be struggling with it. If it were easy, you wouldn't be making mistakes or seeking advice and knowledge. Gaining knowledge and advice isn't a shortcut; it's part of the tough but necessary process of practice. They provide you with the confidence to act.

Just like how my friendship with my overthinking friend led me to overthink for a while, recognizing the need to address and manage overthinking is part of learning and growing.

I realized that when I overthought, I would create false scenarios that made me feel worse and more anxious. On reflection, I saw that I was the one putting myself in these situations, so I was also responsible for my own anxiety and distress. It was like placing myself in a prison and then locking the gate from the outside.

Overthinking is a mental prison where you are both the prisoner and the jailer.

As I continued to figure out ways to overcome overthinking, I realized that the only effective solution is to pause. Stop your mind from creating scenarios. Instead, act decisively and take the right course of action with courage.

Because when you fail to control your thoughts, they end up controlling you. It's almost absurd to be governed by thoughts that you've created yourself. It's like inventing a machine designed to harm threats, only for it to end up harming you instead. Imagine making a groundbreaking innovation and then being undone by it. That's exactly what overthinking does to you.

At its core, overthinking is when you dwell on thoughts and scenarios more than necessary, leading to your own suffering. Essentially, you're responsible for your own distress. Isn't it crazy to be the cause of your own suffering? You're essentially suffering from your own intelligence. Don't let that happen! He concluded.

I Wish I Stayed True to Myself

You've probably heard this line many a times: "Your conscience is your true judge." I regret not listening to it or avoiding it on a few occasions. I regret not staying true to myself.

When you have a watchman outside your building, you sleep peacefully knowing that someone is keeping an eye out for robbers at the gate. The robbers stay away, aware that their attempts to break in might lead to their capture and arrest. If there were no watchman, the building and its occupants would be vulnerable, and the robbers would have the advantage. Similarly, if you lack a watchman for yourself, your conscience or inner moral guide, you are more likely to act without considering the consequences, leaving yourself vulnerable or in a position to cause harm to others.

How can you avoid this? By being true to yourself, by acting as a watchman for your body and mind, and by gatekeeping your actions. You need to tell yourself what's right and what's wrong, what must be done, and what must be avoided. If you try to be a half-hearted watchman and fail to fulfill your duties completely, you risk straying onto the wrong paths. This can lead to misery, regret, or finding yourself on the wrong side of things.

Always act as if God is watching you, observing your thoughts about making wrong decisions, deceiving others, or doing harm, not only to those around you but also to yourself. When you feel watched, you're more likely to act accordingly. If you don't believe in God, then believe in yourself and keep a vigilant eye on your own actions. Ultimately, you can't be an atheist if you live as a godly person who believes in and upholds your own principles.

Imagine a child who is told not to eat candies because they will cause tooth decay. The child might understand this, but does he listen? No. The immediate joy of eating a candy is all he can focus on, and he can't foresee the long-term consequence of tooth decay. Acting for immediate gratification without considering the consequences isn't wise. When the child is under his mother's watchful eye, he refrains from eating the candies. But as soon as she turns her back, the candies are in his mouth.

A child may not be able to watch over himself and might not fully understand the consequences of his actions. However, an adult does have the capacity to understand these consequences but may still fail to stay true to themselves.

Stay true to yourself when no one is watching; if you only act with integrity when you're observed, you are no longer in control of your own actions.

How does this help you? Imagine the same child who, after eating too many candies, ends up with tooth decay and is taken to the dentist. The dentist advises, "If you don't control your candy consumption, your tooth will decay further, and I'll have to extract it." The dentist then looks at the mother and says, "Please ensure the child doesn't have candies frequently."

His mother, concerned for the child, told him that if he refrained from eating candies for the next three months, his toothache would go away, and he could enjoy as many candies as he wanted afterward. Additionally, he would be taken to a fairyland. The child, realizing his mistake, promised his mother he would avoid candies. However, the next day, by lunchtime, the principal called his mother to pick up the boy from school because he was complaining of severe toothache.

The mother rushed to the school to pick up her son and took him to the hospital. The doctor applied pain soothing cream to the tooth and prescribed medication for the rest of the week. They then went home.

The mother asked the child, "Did you eat any candies at school?" The child, filled with regret, nodded his head in acknowledgment of his mistake.

That's when his mother said, "If I can't watch you all the time, it doesn't mean you can't stay true to yourself. Even if your friends offered you candies, you could have stayed true to your commitment. When you stay true to yourself, you will not regret it. The temptation for immediate reward may seem sweet at first, but it will bring pain in the end. Self-control is always rewarding. Understood?" The child nodded, "Yes," but the next day, he ate a candy. As a result, his tooth had to be removed.

"That child was your uncle, your mother's brother!"

When I heard this from my grandpa, I couldn't help but laugh. The mood lightened between us, and I completely forgot that I was having this conversation with him while he was lying in his hospital bed, awaiting surgery.

"Uncle must regret it. Why do you regret it, Grandpa?" I asked in wonder.

"Your uncle didn't just regret it, he learned a hard lesson," Grandpa replied. "After his tooth was removed and his friend made fun of him at school, he never touched a candy again for a long time."

And I'm regretting it because there have been numerous situations in my life where I wasn't true to myself.

When your grandmother asked me to promise her that I would never touch a cigar, I said, 'I promise! I'll never touch it again.' Yet, I didn't stay true to myself or to my promise.

When I told myself I would earn my second degree in arts and communications and work hard every day toward it, I didn't stay true to myself and ended up discontinuing the course.

When I told myself I would buy you a motorbike after saving money, I ended up spending the money on other things and didn't stay true to my promise.

"It's okay, Grandpa! You did so much for me. Do you think I was disappointed? Never!" I immediately tried to reassure him.

"That's the point I'm trying to make," he continued. "It's not about others' expectations of me; it's about my expectations of myself. If I decide to complete or achieve something, only I know about it unless I share it with someone. When I fail to do it, I'm the only one who truly knows I've failed."

Just because the world doesn't know about something I failed at; it doesn't change the fact that I've let myself down. Admitting your mistakes, even when they remain

unknown to the world, is the true measure of staying true to yourself.

"There is one incident I've never revealed to anyone, not even to your grandma, but I'm sharing it with you now. When I was about 13 years old, my friends and I were quite playful. We used to collect cardboards, wooden blocks from the backyards of our houses and build a fire. We'd sit around it, pretending it was a campfire. During the winter season, we would enjoy the warmth of the fire and head back home once it burned out."

Most of the time, the weather would be too windy or cold. The wooden blocks we gathered would either not catch fire or be extinguished by the strong winds. It was a challenging task for us to light the fire and keep it burning for any length of time.

This became a regular practice for us. Matches were like toys, and we wouldn't leave behind a single piece of paper, wooden blocks or cardboard we found in our homes.

One day, my friend tried to light the wooden blocks using a scrap of paper he'd found, but he couldn't get it to catch fire. Frustrated, he started lighting each matchstick and throwing them into the air, venting his anger. I warned him not to do that, especially when he aimed a few matches toward me. We both then slowly began walking back home.

On our way home, we came across a large pile of scrap next to a hut with a roof made of dry grass blocks. My friend continued his practice and threw one of the matches onto the pile. The fire seemed to go out immediately. I suggested he check to see if the fire was really extinguished, but he responded, "The weather is terrible today! Nothing will catch fire," and he took me home without checking to see if the fire was fully out.

We both went home, and after a while, I heard people screaming in panic. I went outside and saw people running toward the scrapyard. I asked my mother what had happened, and she replied, "The scrapyard has caught fire, and the adjacent house is completely burnt." I was shell-shocked and ran back inside my house, not wanting to leave. I was terrified, knowing that my friend and I were responsible for the accident. The villagers later confirmed that a drunkard who used to collect that scrap had perished in the fire inside the hut.

I ran to my friend's place, and he was as terrified as I was. We both went to the scene of the incident to understand what was happening. When we arrived, we saw the hut completely burned down, and the corpse had already been removed. The police had arrived and began investigating, questioning people about what had happened and who might be responsible. It was winter and a windy day, so we couldn't blame the weather. During the investigation, one of the policemen looked at me and said, "You? People say the kids around here play with matches. Did you or any of your friends do this?"

I knew it was my friend who was responsible, but I chose to remain silent. I nodded my head and said, "No," avoiding the truth.

Since the drunkard had no family to come forward, the police eventually closed the case after a few months of investigation. Despite this, I've always felt a deep sense of guilt about the man who died. He was nearly homeless, working at the scrapyard and collecting garbage. My friend's one careless act led to his death in his sleep, and the lack of family meant he never received justice.

Even though my friend was involved, I regret not informing the police about his fault and helping to ensure justice was served. While it might seem unimportant in the grand scheme, viewing the situation from the perspective of the deceased or his potential relatives is haunting.

Sometimes, even if the truth is painful for you or those close to you, it's better to choose honesty over deceit. Lies can haunt you with guilt for a lifetime, while the pain of the truth is only temporary.

When I say I regret not being true to myself, I mean more than just not lying to myself about external situations; I also regret not being honest about my true identity. There are unique attributes and personality traits that define who I am, and I shouldn't be afraid of embracing them as long as I don't hurt others. There were times when I tried to be someone I'm not, and I regret those moments deeply.

I'll share a small incident to illustrate how being yourself can lead you forward. During my college days, I was asked to volunteer with the arts and culture team and collaborate with various colleges and universities across the state to perform at state-level competitions.

The competition encouraged participants from across the state to represent their culture and traditions through various forms of art, including singing, dancing, drawing, and physical exhibitions.

I got the opportunity to join the cultural showcase club, where I was tasked with representing the traditional attire of old tribes. I hesitated during the first practice session, but I later convinced myself to move forward with confidence in what I was doing.

I embraced the role and even crafted an improvised poetry related to that traditional group. After a few practice sessions, I perfected it. The entire committee was pleased with my performance and was eager to see me showcase it on stage during the competition.

However, I was nervous about the attire since it was related to a tribe. It wasn't that I was trying to demean any culture or tradition; it was just that the attire was common to that historical period, and it felt somewhat irrelevant in the present day. I observed the other groups engaged in singing and dancing and found myself drawn to them. I began to feel that I shouldn't continue with my current role and started searching for another role I could take on.

My friends from the western music club looked fantastic with their outfits and instruments during the practice sessions. I asked if I could join them because their performance seemed impressive. However, I soon realized that I couldn't be part of it, as my talent lay elsewhere.

Despite this, I joined the western music club, primarily to look better rather than to genuinely contribute to their performance. However, the tribal dress-up team approached me again, emphasizing that they wouldn't find a better fit for the role and urging me to stay true to myself and what I was good at.

I declined their request and proceeded to join the western music club. However, they needed a replacement for my role, so I persuaded a junior to take over. I had him recite the same poem I had written and improvised for the act. He was confident and unreserved in the traditional attire, and he delivered a stunning performance on the final stage. The judges were very impressed.

In fact, he was awarded second prize at the competition for his authenticity and expressive performance through the attire and dialect.

I regretted that decision deeply when the western club I joined didn't gain any attention, except for the fancy attire we wore. I wasn't even part of the main performance group.

That day, I realized that staying true to yourself and embracing what you're good at, while avoiding the fear of judgment, will lead you forward. The moment you try to be someone you're not just to impress others, you will inevitably fail.

Being true to yourself doesn't mean limiting your potential for improvement or better opportunities. Rather, it involves acknowledging your true identity and avoiding the adoption of something that doesn't align with who you are.

I remember a friend of mine who was known as the most introverted student at the university. He was always shy about expressing his thoughts, despite having a wealth of knowledge. His main area of improvement was overcoming his fear of judgment and speaking out with confidence.

However, any change must be genuine and lasting, not fake and temporary. What I mean is, if he becomes a brave person who isn't afraid to speak his mind, that should be his true personality, not just a façade he puts on for the moment.

Change is inevitable, and while it might start as something you fake initially, it should eventually become a natural part of your personality. It should evolve to align with who you are and reinforce your true self.

If my friend tries to act as the bravest person for just a day, that wouldn't truly represent who he is. Being true to himself involves acknowledging both his strengths and weaknesses.

There was a beautiful girl at the university whom everyone admired and wanted to talk to. However, many of the boys tried to appear overly confident when approaching her, only to be rejected almost immediately because she could sense the artificiality of their approach.

One day, when my introverted friend was passing by, the girl was concerned about how to get to a specific room. Without thinking, she asked my friend for directions.

My friend, true to his shy nature, simply pointed in the direction without saying a word and then left. The girl was surprised by his response. She was used to people taking every opportunity to start a conversation, often with trivial chatter that she found off-putting.

However, when she initiated a conversation this time, my friend didn't respond, nor did he try to prolong it. She found this refreshing and liked it!

The timing proved fortunate, as he was tested multiple times and passed each one effortlessly because he was true to himself. Eventually, the conversation between them began, and to everyone's surprise, they both liked each other. He ended up making the entire university envious.

When most of the boys asked her what it was about him that she liked, which wasn't found in the others, she replied, "He's just being himself. He doesn't try to be someone else to impress me. He is genuine, and that impresses me."

That's how life can be rewarding at times, when you are true to yourself.

While it's essential to always be true to yourself and your personality, there are times when you must not fake it but instead promise to be adaptive.

Being adaptive is different from being fake. Adaptation involves adjusting and altering according to what's required in a specific situation, place, or with a particular person. While it's crucial to be true to yourself, failing to adapt can lead to failure. When you adapt, you don't resist change. By not resisting change, you naturally transform. Even with this transformation, the adjusted personality remains true to your core self.

For example, during an interview, my innocent friend can't be fake or remain exactly as he is. He needs to make a promise about what he can become in order to pursue the job. When he makes that promise and adapts accordingly, he is still being true to himself.

"By welcoming change instead of fighting it, you open yourself to transformation. This journey doesn't reinvent who you are but rather refines and enhances the essence of your true self, helping you become the best version of yourself."

"Are you saying that what I perceive as my weaknesses could actually become my strengths?" I asked my grandpa for his thoughts.

He responded firmly, "No, your weak comprehension skills won't ever be seen as strengths."

He continued, "What it means is that if you stay true to yourself, you'll also be true to others. When people sense that authenticity, they will reward you, either directly or indirectly. That doesn't mean a weakness is permanent, though. For example, the university student whose innocence was endearing wouldn't have been tolerated by his girlfriend if he remained that way forever. He needed to adapt. So, your weakness can never become your strengths but could sometimes open up opportunities to transform yourself."

Acknowledging your weaknesses, rather than pretending they don't exist, is crucial. Trying to hide them might lead to negative consequences. The key is being honest with yourself. Just like you asked me a straightforward question now, though it might seem trivial, your honesty in seeking clarity is valuable. If you had pretended to understand everything, you'd miss out on important lessons.

I scratched my head, unsure whether my grandpa was praising me or subtly calling me foolish. I nodded in agreement and continued to listen, reflecting on his words.

Honesty is always rewarding, even if it isn't evident at the beginning; it will pay off in the long run. On the other hand, dishonesty might bring you immediate rewards but will eventually lead to unavoidable consequences.

I remember a story about a famous entrepreneur and venture capitalist who started with a transportation business and now leads a multinational company. In his early days, not being true to himself landed him in trouble. If I recall correctly, he described it as follows:

"There was a time when my cousin and I were venturing into the agricultural sector with a bold business idea. We aimed to streamline the transportation process by eliminating the numerous intermediaries and commissions that complicated the journey from farm to customer. We decided to pilot this idea in a nearby village and began consulting with farmers to understand their selling process.

Through numerous interactions, we discovered that farmers faced significant delays and costs due to the convoluted approval and transport systems. Our plan was to implement a single transport lane to reduce expenses and time. To move forward, we needed approval from local government bodies and transportation parties affected by our proposal.

During the approval process, a government official suggested that we lie about the impact on transportation bodies to expedite the approval. I questioned the wisdom of this approach, concerned about being held accountable later.

The official's response was blunt: 'If you want your business to succeed, you need to follow my advice,' he said, leaving me with a persistent sense of unease. My cousin echoed his sentiment, urging me to misrepresent our compensation plan for the transporters.

When presenting our proposal, a signing authority asked, 'How will you handle the job losses among the transportation bodies?'

The official who had advised me to lie was present, and as he winked at me, signaling to follow his suggestion, I faced a moral dilemma. I chose to stay true to myself. I acknowledged the authority's concerns and said, 'We don't have a plan yet, but I'll work with the transporters to find alternatives or compensation solutions.'

The authority frowned, visibly disappointed, and the proposal was rejected. My cousin was disheartened, expressing, 'Brother, we could have figured it out eventually. You won't get this chance again.'

Feeling frustrated and defeated, I inquired if anything could be done to rectify the situation. The official offered a solution: pay a commission, and he'd ensure the proposal was reconsidered.

Despite my reluctance, I felt cornered and agreed. Two days later, the proposal was approved after I answered 'yes' when asked if the transport bodies wouldn't be affected.

Though the transport system was efficient and saved time for the farmers, problems arose when local transporters began protesting. The situation escalated when the protesters destroyed the farmers' crops and set our office on fire.

We were held accountable and faced an investigation. The documents showed our assurances that no local transportation bodies would be harmed and that a compensation plan was in place, which was not true. We were placed under interim detention and given a week to work on a compensation plan.

Out on bail, I immediately sought to address the issue. I met with the protesters and requested three months to develop a compensation plan. During this period, I remained true to myself, resisting temptations to bribe officials or blame the protesters.

I sold my properties to compensate those affected and developed a plan to integrate the local transporters into other states where our business was expanding. Over the years, the situation improved. The transportation sector thrived, and the local transporters became integral to our company, generating millions in revenue.

In hindsight, I believe staying true to oneself is the only path to true success. Temptations to take shortcuts or deceive may seem like solutions but often lead to more significant problems. The truth may be harsh, but it acts as a protective shield. Lies, on the other hand, only breed more lies, creating a destructive cycle. Facing the truth and making difficult, honest choices is like navigating through a giant wave, though it might be a severe blow at first, overcoming it prepares you for smoother sailing ahead."

That story of the entrepreneur was always struck with me and every time I was tempted to take the wrong decisions deceiving self, I thought of it and tried to stay true to myself but again I wouldn't have regrets on it if never failed at it.

Nowadays, the demand for influence and motivation is higher than ever. People often don't take the time to reflect on who they truly are or what they genuinely want. Instead, they get swayed by external influences and try to become something they're not.

Before you can determine who, you want to become, it's crucial to understand who you truly are. Many people overlook this important step, focusing instead on questions about their future, what they should be or how they should be. But do you know what you are right now? Understanding your current self is essential for charting a clear path toward your future goals.

While it's important to understand your place in life, seeing someone in a better position can spark a desire to improve yourself or even surpass them. However, if you focus too much on becoming someone else, you risk losing sight of your own identity and the path to becoming a better version of yourself.

To elaborate, imagine you're on a busy street surrounded by high-rise buildings, where people from all over the city come to shop. As you make your way to another street, you notice a crowd gathered around, intently watching a performance or act.

As you approach the group, you see they are all thrilled by a man playing his electric guitar. His skill is remarkable, his hands move so swiftly that they seem almost invisible, and the guitar produces a bass that resonates pleasantly with everyone's eardrums. After the performance, the crowd erupts in joy, applauding and cheering for him, completely captivated by his artistry. Seeing how he captivated the audience with his performance, you decide to buy an electric guitar for yourself, dreaming of one day putting on a show as impressive as the one you just witnessed.

As you continue deeper into the streets, you spot a wealthy man driving his red Ferrari through the crowd. Everyone around is in awe, pulling out their phones to capture the moment. Inspired by the sight, you find yourself dreaming of owning a similar car someday.

As you move ahead, you notice a small child sleeping on the side of the street while her mother tries to sell toys amidst the busy crowds. Looking back, you feel a deep sense of gratitude for what you already have and realize that it's unnecessary to dwell on what you don't possess.

As you continue on, you spot a pair of eye-catching sneakers in a store window. You quickly enter the store to inquire about the price, only to feel a pang of disappointment as you realize you can't afford them for yourself.

As the street comes to an end, you're left with a whirlwind of emotions, wanting to be like someone you saw, feeling discontent with who you are, and being deeply influenced by everything around you. Instead of simply observing, you take everything personally, letting the sights and experiences sway you. In the end, you realize that you were controlled by the external influences on the street, rather than being true to yourself.

So, you buy the guitar and, after trying to learn it for a day, you abandon it. Your dream of owning the red Ferrari fades after just a few days. Your gratitude disappears at the first sign of inconvenience, and everything you've tried to achieve unravels. Each new experience pushes you to become someone else, and if this pattern continues, you might spend your life chasing after fleeting desires, never truly understanding who you were.

While inspirations can be powerful motivators for pursuing goals or dreams, it's crucial to reflect on three key questions:

1. What do I really want?
    Clarify your true desires and aspirations.

2. Why do I want it?
    Understand the underlying reasons and motivations behind your goals.

3. 3. If I don't get it, what will I do?
    Consider how you will respond if you don't achieve your goal and how you'll maintain your sense of purpose or how will it affect your well-being.

By addressing these questions, you can ensure that your pursuits are aligned with your authentic self and not just fleeting influences.

That's it. Ask yourself these three questions before you're influenced or even when you feel you are being influenced.

What do I really want?

Sit down and make a list of one hundred things you'd like to have or achieve in your life over the next five, ten, or fifteen years. Include anything, whether material possessions, relationships, emotions, places, or abstract concepts. Write them all down. If you think one hundred items isn't enough, try listing at least twenty first and notice how challenging it becomes after a certain point. This exercise reveals that your true wants may not be as extensive as you think. Give it a try!

Why do I want it?

This is a crucial question. After you've compiled your list of wants, take the time to analyze each item and determine a solid reason behind it. Ask yourself why you desire each thing. Eliminate those items for which you can't provide a meaningful rationale, perhaps you saw them once and were simply drawn to them, or you think having a particular person in your life would be entertaining. Your reasons need to be personal and substantial. For example, if you still find yourself wanting that red Ferrari you saw on the busy street, and you have a clear, compelling reason for it, then keep it on your list.

If I don't get it, what will I do?

With your trimmed list in hand, review each item once more and ask yourself what you would do if you didn't achieve it. Will you feel intense regret that could disrupt your life? Would not having it make it difficult for you to go on? Will its absence make you feel like a failure? This process will help you identify which desires truly matter to you and which ones can be let go. By understanding the potential impact of not achieving each goal, you can focus on what's genuinely important.

Now, you'll have a final list reflecting your true wants and desires. This list represents your authentic self. When you find yourself influenced or pressured, refer back to this list to stay true to who you are.

If you're uncertain about new desires or influences, apply the same three questions to them: determine what you really want, why you want it, and what you'd do if you don't get it. This will help you decide whether to add it to your final list or remove it from consideration.

While it's fine to have desires without a clear rationale, especially for material things, life doesn't work the same way for emotions, feelings, people, and experiences. These aspects of life often require deeper understanding and meaningful connections rather than just a list of wants.

If everyone could obtain anything they wanted without effort, nothing would hold true value. When you receive something without having to work for it, it loses its sense of accomplishment and may even diminish your appreciation for it. The effort and struggle often give meaning and worth to our achievements.

When you stay true to yourself, your list of desires becomes shorter but more meaningful. While having fewer, genuine goals might initially feel disheartening, achieving them brings a profound sense of fulfillment and success. Conversely, chasing numerous goals that don't truly resonate with you can lead to emptiness, a sense of loss, and disappointment.

I wish I networked more

Imagine if kings had to settle their disputes by dueling one-on-one instead of leading entire armies into battle. What do you think the outcomes would have been? My grandpa asked me.

I said it would have been fantastic, many lives would have been spared. The massive loss of soldiers in countless battles could have been avoided.

He smiled and said, "I agree, but that's not how wars work. Imagine if the king were on the verge of losing; he might call on his ministers, then generals, then soldiers to join the fight until every one of the armies is utilized."

"To make it fair, they'd need to establish strict rules to prevent that from happening." I said in response.

He replied, "If the person enforcing the rules is killed?"

It could lead to chaos and the very thing we're trying to avoid. Maintaining order and fairness would be a constant challenge in wars.

He continued, "Wars don't follow rules. If kings fought one-on-one, here's what would likely happen: a losing king would first call his minister for help, then if needed, the army general, and then the entire army, basically, until the last soldier of the kingdom is involved. No single king would be able to overcome all these reinforcements. And guess what? The other king would do the same. In the end, the wars would play out as they always have, not between individual kings, but between entire kingdoms, armies, and teams."

"Now you see," he continued, "no war can be won alone. Unless you're up against someone who's completely alone, you need an army. You need kings, ministers, army generals, and soldiers. Every single one of them plays a crucial role."

"Life is much the same," he added. "At each stage, you need people around you who know you well and whom you know well. They serve as your support and, in turn, you serve as theirs. Just like in a war, the people who join you will have different roles at different times, sometimes as kings, sometimes as ministers, and sometimes as army generals. Their roles and contributions will vary, but each one is important to your journey."

"That's what networking is all about," he said. "People often overlook its importance and don't engage in it as much as they should. In today's world, networking isn't about ministers or soldiers, nor is it about winning wars or defeating opponents. It's about uplifting each other, standing by each other when needed, and navigating through life and the systems we've developed.

Can you navigate all alone? Probably, yes, but it would be incredibly challenging. Imagine being asked to steer a massive ship through a stormy sea all by yourself. You'd be the captain, the deckhand, the navigator, the repair person, the anchor operator, and the caretaker of the passengers, all at once. Would it be an easy journey or a difficult one?"

"A difficult one," I replied, understanding his point.

Exactly! Now, imagine that ship has a full crew. Each person has a different role, whether it's steering the ship or cleaning it. When everyone focuses on their own tasks, the whole operation runs smoothly. That's how networking works. It is needed when you're set out to sail bigger ships or missions in your life or at times even when you just need that hand to rescue.

When you're cleaning the ship, you're supporting the person steering it, so they don't have to worry about the cleanliness of the ship. In turn, the steerer is supporting you by ensuring the ship reaches its destination without you having to focus on navigation. Each person plays their part, creating a seamless partnership where everyone can concentrate on their own responsibilities, knowing others are handling theirs.

I regret not networking more. It's not just about making my own life easier; it's also about how I could have made things easier for others. Let me share four major events from my life to illustrate this better.

During my teenage years, my friends and I went for an evening walk, chatting and joking about various events in our lives, just like any group of friends. However, the conversation between two of my friends started to escalate and become personal. I noticed the tension and tried to defuse the situation, hoping to calm things down. Despite my efforts, they ignored me and continued to argue. What started as a heated debate quickly spiraled into a verbal clash and then into a physical altercation.

One of them ended up knocking the other to the ground. When the fight broke out, most of the friends quickly scattered, leaving only three or four of us still at the scene.

When I tried to help the friend who had fallen to the ground, I lifted him by the back of his head and tried to wake him up.

I noticed my hands were covered in blood. I carefully positioned him sitting up and asked someone nearby to get me some water. By then, the friend who had started the fight had run off, likely afraid of the consequences.

I was in a tough spot. Although I hadn't been involved in the fight, I couldn't just leave him there. I knew I'd never forgive myself if something happened to him because I abandoned him. I tried to clean his face and wound, and woke him slightly. He opened his eyes but couldn't speak. The bleeding worsened, and I saw a small piece of glass from a broken soda bottle embedded in his head. I quickly arranged for him to be taken to a nearby hospital and rushed to his home to inform his parents. When I got there, I found their house locked and no one home.

I assumed they might be out somewhere, so I informed the neighbors about the situation and gave them the hospital details. I decided to go home for a bit and either return to check on the friends or visit the hospital again later.

When I got home, I saw my parents at the gate talking to two policemen. I approached them, trying to understand what was going on. As I neared, one of the officers looked at me and said, 'Aren't you the one breaking people's heads on the road?' I was stunned and replied, 'What? Sir, I was just helping my friend and joined him at the hospital.' The police officer responded, 'We know who did what. Let us handle the situation and determine who is at fault.'

I realized what had happened. The person who had beaten up my friend was trying to avoid facing consequences and had shifted the blame onto me. I was taken to the police station and questioned about the incident. Initially, the officers were skeptical of my account and asked me to remain there until further notice.

I spent the whole night waiting on a bench at the police station, hoping someone would eventually tell me, 'You can go now!' I ended up falling asleep there. The next morning, I woke up to see my parents and my friend's father talking to the police. His father, who worked as a magistrate and had connections within the police department, had come to help.

When he explained what had happened, the police were more receptive and took swift action to identify the true culprit also after talking to my other friends who were there at the incident. It struck me that while my own account had been met with skepticism because they didn't know me, my friend's father's version was taken seriously because of his established connections.

That experience made me regret not having any personal connections within the police force. I realized how valuable it could be to have such connections. Whether it's for clearing up misunderstandings, dealing with emergencies, or resolving issues, knowing someone in law enforcement can make a significant difference. It's not that the police don't do their job for the public, but having a personal connection often means things get handled more quickly and effectively.

Let me tell you about another incident from my adult life. When I started my first job, I wanted to buy a piece of land but couldn't afford it. As time went on, and after getting married and having kids, I saved up money for their future. After a few years, I realized that my savings might not be enough, so I decided to invest them to grow my wealth. Buying land seemed like a great idea, especially since it was something I had always wanted to do.

I consulted several real estate agents and eventually found a small piece of land on the outskirts of town. It was ideal for potentially building a home for my family. I used most of my savings to purchase it and completed all the legal paperwork.

For the first few years, I didn't do anything with the land. But when I saw that land prices had risen, I thought selling it for a profit would be better than investing more money into building a house. Just as I was about to put it up for sale, I discovered that the person who sold me the land had a documented promise to transfer it to his son after his death, a detail he had not disclosed to me.

Although the legal paperwork I had seemed in order, and there had been no need for the son's signature at the time of sale, the son demanded the return of the land. I firmly objected, stating that I had purchased it legally and had all the necessary documentation to prove it.

But things didn't turn out in my favor. The son had connections with a prominent lawyer in town and was willing to spend a fortune to secure the land, knowing that the land's high market value would still leave him with a substantial profit. I was disheartened and didn't want to hire a lawyer myself, as I had already invested most of my savings into the land and hadn't saved up much since, due to family expenses.

Many friends advised against a legal battle, suggesting it would be a lengthy and costly process with uncertain outcomes. Despite this, I tried to find a lawyer who could represent me for a lower fee. However, I couldn't find anyone willing to take the case at a reduced rate.

With no viable legal options and no way to afford a lawyer, I had no choice but to settle with the son. He agreed to compensate me with an amount close to what I originally paid for the land. While it wasn't a great deal, it was the only option available to me. I ended up incurring a loss instead of making the significant profit I had hoped for.

Reflecting on it, I regret not having personal connections with any lawyers who could have represented me at a lower cost. If I had known someone in the legal field, I might have been able to fight for my rights and potentially secure a better outcome, even if it took years. It was a hard lesson in the value of networking.

Here's another story from when I moved to a new city for my job. It took me some time to get settled and adjust to the new environment. I asked my parents to come and support my wife, as she was the only one who knew nobody but me in this new town. When they visited, I noticed my father was experiencing severe chest pain and persistent headaches. He downplayed it, saying it was just stress and part of the adjustment process, but I was concerned.

Without a network of doctors in this new city, I felt uncertain about how to proceed. When my father's pain persisted, I took him to a nearby medical consultancy. The doctor examined him and suggested it might be physical stress, recommending rest, some tablets, and exercise. Although my father followed the advice, his condition worsened, and he was in so much pain that we decided to return to our town for treatment.

Upon getting a second opinion from a doctor back home, it was revealed that my father had coronary artery disease and needed immediate surgery. Unfortunately, he passed away a few months after the operation. The doctor explained that early detection and treatment could have made a significant difference.

If I had known any doctors personally in the new city, someone who would have genuinely invested time in diagnosing the issue accurately rather than just prescribing medications, I might have been able to get my father the help he needed sooner. It was a painful lesson in how crucial personal connections can be in critical situations.

Networking isn't about having a vast, uncontrolled web of connections. Instead, it's about cultivating a manageable and reliable set of relationships. It's not about knowing thousands of people but having a few trusted contacts whom you can rely on anytime. Quality matters more than quantity.

If you feel you haven't networked much in your life, the next step isn't to try and befriend everyone you meet.

In fact, knowing too many people can be less effective than having no connections at all. Focus on building a smaller, more meaningful network where relationships are genuine and supportive.

When you know too many people, you not only have an overwhelming number of potential solutions to manage but also face a multitude of problems to address. To build a strong network, you should focus on quality over quantity. Instead of trying to connect with everyone, concentrate on nurturing deeper relationships with a selected few who can genuinely support you and whom you can rely on.

Create a strong-level network by structuring your relationships into a strong matrix. Cultivate deep connections with a select group of people, offering help when you can, so they will be there for you when you need them.

Develop a mid-level matrix with individuals you stay in touch with occasionally. You don't need to have regular conversations or respond to every call, but maintaining some contact can be beneficial. They might assist you in times of need, though the level of support isn't guaranteed.

Lastly, build a low-level matrix where you recognize and remember people when you encounter them. Engage in meaningful conversations to identify those who might move up to a higher level in your network. This way, you keep your connections organized and effective.

Strong-Level Matrix: Cultivate deep connections; offer help to build trust.
Mid-Level Matrix: Maintain occasional contact; stay connected for potential support.
Low-Level Matrix: Engage meaningfully; identify potential connections for growth.

Networking is about surrounding yourself with people who can contribute meaningfully. Take, for example, the movie

300. The Spartan king leads with just three hundred highly skilled soldiers, while the other king, whom he encounters, brings a larger number of less relevant professionals, sculptors, painters, and others to the battlefield.

In the end, it's the Spartan king and his specialized, reliable network that triumph.

This illustrates that having a well-connected, capable team can be far more effective than simply having a larger quantity of less relevant connections.

Another common misconception is that people in your strong matrix, the ones with whom you've built deep relationships will always come through for you and lead you to success. While they are reliable and valuable, networking can also involve momentary connections.

These fleeting relationships might not be based on established trust but rather on the immediate appeal of your ideas, statements, or circumstances. Trust and deeper connections are often built over time, based on the outcomes of these initial interactions. Therefore, it's crucial to seize these opportunities, as they can lead to meaningful relationships and future support.

When I ran up to my favorite actor on a movie set and excitedly declared, 'I want to be an actor like you someday!' The actor responded by telling me to prove myself when he returned to town next. He didn't know me or my family, nor did he have any trust in me as a person. His trust was in my enthusiasm and the sincerity of my statement.

The actor may not have known exactly why he decided to look for me the next time he was in town or why he promised me a chance if I proved myself. It simply happened because I took the opportunity to network. Networking isn't always about established, long-term relationships; it can also be about seizing the moment to present yourself, interact, and make a first impression. If it works out, you have a successful network; if not, it's simply an attempt.

Trying is never wrong, no matter the time or place.

For instance, there was a woman in New York who lost her high-paying job due to company reorganization and cost-cutting. With a husband earning only a small wage and two children to care for, she faced a challenging situation.

The tough times put her family in a difficult position. She diligently applied for hundreds of jobs daily but received no responses from recruiters. She also networked extensively with friends of friends on professional platforms, seeking referrals and any job opportunities. Despite being open to positions for which she was overqualified or that paid less than her previous salary, no immediate opportunities materialized.

She was utterly devastated and anxious about her situation. On her way home after an interview, she didn't get selected for, she took a moment to observe the city around her. She watched the people and the places, searching for a twinkle of hope and trying to assemble the courage to keep trying.

As she walked down a narrow street, she noticed a crowd gathered nearby. Curious, she approached the gathering and saw that it was centered around a poster from one of the newly opened pizza chain restaurants in the city.

They were running a campaign to attract customers, offering a 50% discount on orders for those who scanned a code using their mobile app. People were eagerly rushing to capture the barcode on their phones, as only the first hundred scans would be deemed valid, and the rest would be invalid.

She found the campaign fascinating and realized the importance of marketing a product effectively, even offline, in an age where everything seems to be online. When she got home, she checked her various online platforms and networks, hoping for a lead or connection that could help her. Unfortunately, as usual, she found none that could offer the assistance she needed.

Before she went to sleep, she lay awake, staring at the ceiling. Her husband noticed and asked, "What's wrong? Are you worried about your job?"

She quietly shook her head and replied that she had an idea but wasn't sure if people would think she was mad for pursuing it. Her husband pressed for details, asking,

"What's the idea?"

She responded, "I don't know yet. Let me execute it first, and then I'll tell you how it goes."

He nodded in understanding and went to sleep.

The next day, the woman printed a hundred copies of her resume and walked through the industrial areas where many corporate companies were located. She began posting her resumes on the walls, much like the posters for the pizza chain, hoping to catch the attention of potential employers.

She continued this effort throughout the day, covering various areas and sticking her resumes on walls where they would be clearly visible. On each resume, she had provided her email address, inviting anyone who found a suitable opportunity to contact her.

Her resumes caught the attention of many people across different companies in the corporate areas. Reactions varied, some found it amusing, others saw it as innovative, and a few considered it illogical. However, most people noticed her effort.

To share their reactions, many posted about her unconventional approach on social media and networking platforms, and it quickly went viral. As a result, she began receiving numerous offers and opportunities.

Among them, the director of a leading marketing company admired her bold and direct approach. Believing she would be a perfect fit for an open marketing manager position, he reached out to her with an offer.

He contacted her via the email address she had provided, and after assessing her through interviews, he was impressed by both her profile and her innovative approach. He offered her the marketing manager position with a very attractive salary.

During an interview with a news channel about how she came up with the idea and her thoughts on landing a job through this unconventional method, she responded:

I firmly believed in the value of offline marketing, recognizing that despite the dominance of the online world, there was still significant potential in reaching people through traditional methods. After struggling to gain traction online, I made a bold decision to distribute my resume throughout the city, hoping that this direct approach would catch someone's attention and lead to a valuable opportunity.

She explained, "Networking isn't just about having thousands of connections who might not help you when you need it. Networking can occur at any time and in any place. It's not necessary for someone to know you for a long time to offer assistance. What matters is that your idea resonates and your need is understood. The director who eventually offered me the job didn't know me personally beforehand, but he appreciated my approach and recognized the potential in my idea. My network wasn't built over years; it was formed in a moment based on the value of my proposal and will serve as a starting point for a stronger network. So, never overlook opportunities, conversations, or actions that might be new to you, these could lead to unexpected and valuable outcomes."

"That was great, Grandpa! Sometimes, I feel like I should seize those opportunities to present my ideas to influential people I see at events or parties, but I hesitate and don't dare to approach them," I said after listening to his insights.

He replied, "That's because you're afraid of rejection. But remember, rejection is often a step toward approval. It helps you refine and improve yourself. So next time, take a chance!"

He continued, "There are some smart people who don't just find opportunities but actively create them to network with others."

I asked, "How?"

He replied, "There was a plumber who lived adjacent to a wealthy neighborhood. Although he had a decent income, the neighborhood was so well-maintained that he rarely had opportunities to do repair work there. Most of his work took him to other areas. He had a passion towards entrepreneurship but wasn't sure how and where to start."

Every time he went to the less affluent areas for work, he couldn't help but feel disheartened. The work often came with lower pay, and he felt it didn't reflect his skills or aspirations.

After a few days of this, he decided to approach the wealthy neighborhood and offer his services voluntarily, hoping to find some work. Unfortunately, none of the residents had any immediate need for his services. As he was returning home, he looked around at the luxurious cars, grand houses, and the opulent lifestyle of the people in that area. He was deeply impressed and began to imagine how much he could potentially earn if he could secure work in such a prosperous neighborhood.

So, he came up with a bold idea. He decided to cut the pipeline that connected the back of the homes to the underground water pumps. A small leak would require repair, and no one would likely question the cause. He went ahead with his plan.

When the family noticed the malfunction in the pipeline system, they quickly called the security. The security team contacted the plumber, who had just been wandering the neighborhood looking for work.

The plumber ended up getting a job at the wealthy house and received a generous tip for his services. While working, he struck up a conversation with the homeowner and discovered that he ran a business in the supply chain industry. The plumber discussed the business with him and exchanged contact information and visiting cards.

After finishing the job and leaving the house, the plumber made another cut in the pipe at a different location. This cut was smaller and would take a few days to develop into a noticeable problem. His plan was to ensure a future opportunity to return and offer his services again.

And, as expected, he was called back again. The homeowner, frustrated and perplexed, complained about the recurring issue with the pipeline, insisting that such problems had never occurred before.

The plumber, feigning concern, suggested that the pipelines might be old and in need of a thorough examination. He proceeded to inspect the pipes, finding no actual problems, but still charged a high fee for his services.

While pretending to examine the pipes, the plumber began discussing his idea of supplying pipeline systems and highlighted the scarcity of quality pipelines in other parts of the city.

The homeowner responded, "I understand, but we're looking for a partner who knows the exact requirements and is familiar with the area better."

The plumber replied, "I've been to every house in that locality. I know exactly which pipelines are needed, how much they can afford, and every detail you might require. I can provide all that information."

Surprisingly, the owner said, "That could be very helpful. Come to my office when you're free this week."

The plumber responded, "I'm actually busy until the end of the week, but I can make it early Monday next week." He used this to create a sense of occupancy and not showcase his desperation or availability.

The owner agreed, and the plumber spent the week gathering more detailed information on pipeline systems. When he met the owner on Monday with his comprehensive report, the owner was impressed and proposed a partnership to develop a plan for the supply chain.

The plumber replied, "I'd be interested in that, but I need some formal education to understand the business basics better."

The owner said, "You can figure it out. If you manage to close this project successfully, here's how much you'll be paid." He then outlined the potential earnings, which left the plumber stunned.

The plumber quickly replied, "I'm definitely in."

The owner continued, "You'll need to gain some lessons on business basics before you can start. There's a tenant in one of our apartments who offers business classes for aspiring learners, although he charges quite a bit."

The plumber nodded and said, "I'll consult with him," then left for the apartment. Once there, he took out his sharp knife and cut the pipeline connected to the tenant's apartment.

We both laughed as my grandpa wrapped up the story of the plumber. He then said, "Sometimes, you don't wait for the knock on the door; you have to plunge through it with force. Whether it's an opportunity or building your network, you have to take decisive action."

I replied, "That sounds great, but I really wonder if there are any set of guidelines or best practices for networking."

He said, "There aren't any universal guidelines. You have to find what works best for you and adapt as you go along."

"I can share a few based on my regrets, experiences, and lessons," he said. "These principles apply to networking in general, though not every network will respond the same way."

Golden Rules for Networking:

#1 Never Force a Conversation: A forced idea or statement won't resonate well; even if it does, it will be quickly forgotten. Let conversations flow naturally.

#2 Dress According to Your Need: Dress in a way that reflects your current objective. If you're seeking help, look like you need it. If you're seeking investment, present yourself as someone with a solid business idea. Job hunting? Dress formally. Align your appearance with the situation and the expectations of your network.

#3 Be Innovatively Memorable: Stand out with creativity, but avoid going overboard. Your goal is to be remembered, not to appear foolish. Find a balance between innovation and appropriateness to leave a lasting impression.

#4 Show Interest in Their Interests: Even if you don't share their likes, show genuine curiosity and enthusiasm for their passions. Align yourself with their interests to build rapport. Being rigidly honest or blunt isn't always effective; sometimes, it's about fitting in and finding common ground.

#5 Start Strong, Navigate the Middle, End Well: Aim to make a powerful first impression and conclude on a positive note. While the middle part of the conversation might blur over time, a memorable beginning and ending leave a lasting impact and make your interaction more memorable.

#6 Handle Uncertain Answers Wisely: If you're unsure about an answer, gauge its importance. For crucial questions, craft a thoughtful response based on your best understanding. For less critical queries, it's okay to take time and follow up later. This approach helps preserve relationships and shows that you value the conversation.

#7 Be Humble, Not Submissive or Desperate: Display humility and confidence without coming across as desperate or submissive. Desperation can be a deterrent, while excessive submission may signal weakness. Balance humility with assertiveness to build a positive impression.

#8 Support Emotion with Reason: Combine emotional appeal with logical arguments. While emotions can drive connection and empathy, they need to be supported by solid reasoning to be truly persuasive. This combination can help in gaining support and making your case more compelling.

#9 Highlight Their Benefits: Focus on what the other person stands to gain from the relationship. Networking is often driven by mutual benefits, so clearly articulate how your proposal or idea can benefit them. If they perceive value in the relationship, they're more likely to engage positively.

#10 Allow for Negotiation: Avoid agreeing to everything out of fear of rejection. Instead, be open to negotiation and seek compromises that benefit both parties. Negotiation is essential for achieving balanced and mutually advantageous outcomes, ensuring that all involved parties feel valued.

I wish I realized the Time is limited.

Like everyone else, I knew that time is irreversible and it won't stop for anyone. But I always thought I had time when I wanted to do something. Whenever I made plans, I'd leave them at the planning stage, convinced that there was always enough time to act. I told myself maybe I was too old or too young for certain things. But it's not about age, it's about how badly you want to do certain things, how quickly the time would pass by.

Like me, you might have hundreds of thoughts swirling in your head right now, about your career, your life, cars, your house, friends, and more. It's true that making wise decisions is crucial, and knowing what to do and what to avoid is important. However, when something feels like it must be done, regardless of the outcome, never tell yourself, "I still have time."

No! you don't. Your mother, your friends, or people around you might say otherwise, but the truth remains the same. Don't listen to them. Listen to the one who is nearing the end of his life, who have seen the entirety of their days pass by. Human life is fleeting, and the notion of "you have time" becomes irrelevant when you look at the bigger picture. You might have time to buy a car or a house, but you don't have unlimited time for everything else. Believing that you have time is not always a wise or acceptable mindset. When you progress with the idea of having more time for yourself, you'll actually run out of time for everything including for those you thought you had enough time.

I replied, "But Grandpa! your daughter always tells me that I shouldn't rush things and should wait for the right time for the right things to happen. I thought that was your teaching to her. Are you saying you regret that now?"

Rushing towards something is different from doing things on time. When I say you must realize you have less time, I don't mean to live each day as if it's your last. Certainly, some things happen at the right time, as your mother says, but you should never waste opportunities assuming you've got plenty of time. Don't procrastinate tasks that can be done now. When I say you have less time, I mean you have a limited span to accomplish what's needed and in today's world everything is needed in amounts more than you thought you'd need. If something can be done now, do it. Don't wait.

"Right, Grandpa!" I said, accepting his point. "But what did you not do on time that's making you regret it now?" I asked, confused.

"Many! Countless situations. I remember when I was young, back in those days, people invested in real estate. The land was vast and people were fewer in my time. I always told myself I would buy some land, thinking it would yield a profit as I got older. I had just enough to make the purchase, but I kept thinking, 'I have time. I'm young now." And I purchased in the later days incurring losses."

"That's a mistake you might think," he continued. "You might say I'm regretting it just because prices went up later, but that's not the case. The money I saved for it didn't stay with me because I kept assuming I had time. I neither spent it wisely nor benefited from it. Even if land prices had dropped,

I wouldn't have lost everything. At some point, I'd have made a profit. But I listened to people who said, 'You're the first one to talk about investing in real estate at your age! This is the time to learn and have fun. You've got time!' Maybe I shouldn't have listened to them."

"What else?" I asked, curiosity piqued.

"Time is a complex concept to grasp," he said. "We've made it into something quantifiable with numbers and clock hands, but it's really just the passing of days and nights. After some days and nights, life ends, and it feels to me like these could be my last days. Do you realize how quickly time slips away?

Consider this: The Earth is around 4 billion years old. How hard is it to fathom that? Yet, the average human lifespan is only about 70 years. Do you see now how limited our time truly is?"

"True, Grandpa," I said. "If God had designed human lives to be immortal, we would age with the Earth and stay here forever."

"In that case," he replied, "you'd want time to pass faster and reach the end sooner."

I looked at him in wonder, as if I didn't quite grasp his perspective. He continued, "The beauty of life lies in its impermanence. If there were no death, you'd be an eternal prisoner on this planet with no release. You'd want to leave but could never escape. Your soul would be trapped in your body forever. And what would drive a person if they knew they had all the time in the world? The concept of time would lose its meaning because you'd be here indefinitely. If you keep telling yourself 'Forever,' you might end up putting things off for thousands of years. Humans tend to procrastinate as if they have endless time."

"This feels too complex to understand," I replied. "I wish time had never been invented."

"Time always existed," he said. "It's abstract; numbers just help us measure it. Even if we hadn't developed the ability to quantify it, we would still age, days and nights would alternate, and eventually, we would die."

"So, you're saying that, overall, life is short and that I have less time than I think I do. Is that right?" I asked, my curiosity growing.

"Almost correct," he said. "If you're not caught off guard by life's unpredictability and find yourself challenged when you least expect it, then your time isn't just less than you comprehend, it's less than you think you have. It's even shorter than that."

"I had a friend from my college days who was very dear to me and the most optimistic person I've ever met. He was always carefree and never seemed to fear the future. While we were all panicking about managing expenses and finding a job after graduation, he remained remarkably calm and never showed any anxiety. I used to ask him, 'Why don't you ever panic?' He would reply, 'Things will happen as they are destined to happen; you can't change what's in your fate.'"

While what he said made absolute sense to me, I still wasn't entirely satisfied with his answer. I wondered if maybe I was too anxious about the future or whether it was okay to make wise decisions before it's too late. Sometimes, I looked at him and felt a pang of jealousy, such a happy man who seemed to believe he had all the time in the world.

When I was invited to his home for lunch, I was surprised by his family's condition. His mother was bedridden, and his father barely earned enough to get by. Despite these challenging circumstances, my friend remained carefree. This was a profound life lesson for me.

I had curious questions swirling in my mind. If I overthink and plan every detail, becoming anxious about the future, I end up robbing myself of the present. Conversely, if I am carefree and not worried about tomorrow, I may face anxiety in the future. Either way, it seemed I was bound to suffer, either in the present or the future.

So, I looked at my friend and asked him the same question. He replied, "I have many plans and I do want to execute them, but not right now. This is my time to be carefree. I don't want to stress over things that would ruin my present."

That hit me hard, and I found myself embracing his philosophy for a while. I asked him, "So you're aware of your mother's condition and your father's earnings? You also have plans you want to execute but are waiting for the 'right time,' aren't you?"

"You got me right, my friend!" he said with a grin. Then he asked if I wanted to join him for a swim in the river outside the town. I thought to myself, "Yeah, things can wait," and agreed to go along with him.

He was as mischievous as he was carefree. We both waded into the river, splashing water at each other. The river was shallow, with mud at the bottom. We played around, diving deep to scoop up mud and stones, and threw them at each other. After he turned my head into a mud mess, he decided to leap off a large rock that looked like a mini mountain, perfect for diving.

Knowing he'd make me dirty again when he returned to the pond, I quickly washed off the mud from my head and brushed the stains from my hands. I hurried out of the pond and started running. As I was making my way back, I heard a splash, confirming that he had jumped into the water with a big dive.

I didn't look back and ran straight home. I took a bath, wrote a few letters, had a small meal, and then fell asleep.

A few hours later, I was jolted awake by a knock on the door. It was another friend, standing there with tear-streaked eyes, trembling hands, and an expression of deep tension.

"Calm down," I said, concerned. "What happened? Is everything okay?"

"He—he's been found dead in the pond," my friend stammered, his voice breaking. "His feet were stuck in the mud, and no one was there to rescue him. His family told you both went swimming together."

I was shell-shocked and devastated. I had never imagined something like this could happen. I had run away after hearing the splash, the final dive of my friend, and couldn't save him. The weight of my regret has stayed with me ever since.

"But it wasn't entirely my fault either," my grandpa continued. "I couldn't return to a normal state for days after the incident. I kept thinking about how my friend believed he had all the time in the world. He had plans that could have helped his family, but he always thought he would get to them later. That 'later' never came."

There was a moment of silence following my grandfather's narrative.

I softly replied, "Grandpa, that doesn't mean everyone dies sooner than they expect. If your friend had lived, he would have had the chance to act on his plans when he thought the time was right, and things might have turned out differently."

My grandfather looked at me, disappointed. "This entire narrative was meant to challenge that very thought, and yet you've come to the same conclusion. Even if my friend hadn't died, the right time for him to act was when he was in a good position to do so, not when he kept telling himself he'd wait for the perfect moment. The right time is always now, not when the moment finally arrives."

"Life is unpredictable," my grandfather said. "These days, especially, I don't see many people living their lives to the fullest. The circumstances are different now, air and water are polluted, and the food isn't as healthy. You never know what might happen at any moment. Life passes faster than you realize, and you could find yourself on your deathbed without having taken any meaningful actions."

"If you have an idea, execute it now.

If you want to start a business, start it now.

If you want to sing a song, sing it loud and clear, now.

If you want to do something important, do it now."

Planning is an essential part of completing a task, but action is even more crucial. Your life shouldn't get stuck in the planning stage, nor should it linger too long in the action stage. Plan your tasks, start executing them, remember, you have less time than you think you do.

Although time may seem limited, we must act more quickly. Time has always been kind to us. Think about it: when you're bored, having a bad day, or when everything feels off, time seems to drag. You often hear people say, 'This week has been so slow,' 'Today was the slowest day of my life,' or 'An hour feels like a day today.'"

"Conversely, when you're extremely happy, whether you're with someone you enjoy being with, hanging out with friends, watching a great movie, or engrossed in a Netflix series, time flies by. You might even find yourself anxious that it's passing too quickly."

"Why does this happen? Time has always been the same, one second is a second, and one hour is an hour. The only difference is that when you're engaged in something you love, you lose track of time and don't realize how long you've been enjoying it. On the other hand, when you're doing something, you dislike, you find yourself checking the clock every five minutes, wondering why it hasn't been an hour already."

"When you need to get things done, approach them with the conviction as if you genuinely want to complete them, regardless of how you feel about them. The time will pass quickly.

Next time, if your Sunday feels short and your Monday seems long, try doing something you don't enjoy but need to do on both days. Initially, both days might feel longer. However, if you practice tackling tasks with conviction, regardless of your feelings, time will not seem faster or slower but will move at its natural pace. This approach will help you feel like you have enough time to accomplish everything in a timely manner."

"I've encountered many situations where I told myself, 'I wish I had more time for this,' 'I wish I had time to get these things done,' or 'I wish I had time for myself,' without realizing that the time was there all along, but I wasted it."

For instance, at my office, there was a book readers' club. I had planned to start reading regularly and make it a habit so I could contribute to the discussions and feel more intellectual. I always wanted to do it. I kept telling myself I needed to start reading books and make it a habit. I bought a book, read two pages on the first day, and then set it aside for 'upcoming days.'

I skipped reading the book the next day, then the week, and eventually the entire month. When I questioned myself about why I hadn't kept up with it, I told myself, 'I just don't have enough time.'

I had work at the office, groceries to buy, family to take care of, time to spend with my children and wife, news to watch, and by the end of the day, I needed time to rest as well.

Ultimately, these excuses prevented me from developing a reading habit, and I never managed to join the readers' club at the office. Eventually, I managed to overcome this mindset and developed a reading habit after a few years, becoming an avid reader.

In retrospect, I always yearned for more time and often begged for it, but when I finally had it, I squandered it. After work, I would go out with my colleagues to the club, spending time playing cards and chatting about trivial matters. By the time I got home, I'd sit and watch TV for the news, then drift into music and movies, spending an hour or so until I'd start yawning and fall asleep. On weekends, I would go out clubbing, tackle household chores, and use any remaining time to rest.

All that time could have been used to pursue my dream of reading books. I could have skipped going to the club, if not every day, at least two or three times a week. I could have turned off the TV after the news, skipped clubbing on weekends, and sacrificed a few hours of sleep. Eventually, I could have developed a reading habit. Those two pages could have turned into hundreds, leading to a series of books. But instead, I chose to waste it.

"Time is what we desire most but squander the most."

"What do you do when you buy a new watch?" my grandpa asked.

"I'd check if it fits, make sure it's working properly, and adjust the time," I replied.

"What do you mean by adjusting the time?" he asked.

"I'd make sure it's set to the correct time and adjust it if it's not."

"Exactly," he said. "But can you adjust it if the time has already passed? You can't. Time is irreversible. Once a moment has passed, it can't be brought back, no matter what. You can only adjust the time if the watch isn't functioning properly but that doesn't allow you to go back and correct things that were done or redo things that were left undone. If it's bygone, it's bygone."

Someone dear to me once said that when someone says, 'I don't have time to do a certain thing,' it really means they don't want to do it. That might sound harsh, but I've come to realize it's true.

If you truly wanted to do something, you would find a way to make time for it. You'd sacrifice time with friends, sleep, scrolling through your phone, or even eating, if necessary. You'd find a way to make it happen.

If you genuinely want to do something, you'll make time for it, even if you're occupied every minute of the day. You'd find at least fifteen minutes to dedicate to it.

Time is limited, but you can still make the most of it. Don't wait for the 'right time,' because by the time it arrives, it might be too late, and you'll be left with nothing but regret, which only wastes more time.

There was a man who perpetually felt his life was slipping away, haunted by the belief that he had too little time. Although he sensed the fleeting nature of his existence, he never understood the crucial truth: he had squandered the time he had, never using it to its full potential. His constant refrain was, 'I have no time.'

When death finally arrived and he found himself in Hell, he was taken aback. "I've never harmed anyone or committed any evil deeds," he protested. "Why am I here? Shouldn't I be in Heaven?"

A demon, draped in shadows, replied with a solemn tone, "You were meant for Heaven, but you were sent here because you failed one crucial criterion: you wasted too much of your time."

The man, bewildered, retorted, "Wasted time? My days were packed with responsibilities and tasks. How could they say I wasted time when I barely had any to spare?"

With an unnerving calm, the demon handed him an ornate calculator. "Enter your date of birth and date of death into this device. It will reveal the truth about your time usage."

The man, both curious and apprehensive, entered his birth date, April 30, 1953, and his death date, June 23, 2024. He pressed Enter, and the calculator whirred to life, quickly processing the data.

The results appeared before him:

- Total days lived: 25,986

- Days awake = Total days – Total days sleeping: 16,241

- Days after deducting time for daily activities: 12,993

- Days after deducting working hours: 5,331

- Days after deducting time for vacation, personal pursuits, family, friends, and entertainment: 2,332

- Total days of time wasted: 1,839

- Total hours of time wasted: 44,136

- Total hours needed to achieve success and meet goals: 35,221

- Difference: 8,915

The man stared in shock. To meet his goals and achieve success, he would have needed 35,221 hours. Yet, he had squandered 44,136 hours. Even if he had used the necessary 35,221 hours efficiently, he would still have had 8,915 hours of idle time left over.

The revelation struck him with a profound clarity. He had wasted so much time, not by making sacrifices, but from the hours he had left after fulfilling all his activities. Had he made even small adjustments to his sleep, vacations, or leisure, he could have set grander goals and transformed his life in ways he had never imagined.

Overwhelmed with regret, the man finally understood the gravity of his mistake. The weight of his squandered time became a burden too heavy to bear, and he accepted his fate in Hell with a sorrowful resignation.

"Holy moly!" I exclaimed, reflecting on how many hours I had already wasted that could have been used more productively. "From today, I'll stop hanging out with friends and cut off all the entertainment. I'm going to focus solely on the important things in my life."

My grandpa chuckled softly and said, "The hours wasted aren't just about cutting out entertainment and happy times.

While it's great that you recognize the need to not waste time, you don't have to be so sacrificial either. Remember, time spent enjoying yourself is not time wasted. However, if you focus too much on small pleasures, you might miss out on bigger opportunities. Sometimes sacrifices are necessary, and sometimes they aren't worth it. You need to find the right balance!"

"If you observe life closely, you'll realize that you're not part of the universe or on this planet forever. Your existence isn't spread across all time but is just a brief moment between two points. So, time isn't moving forward for you; it's more accurate to say that you're running out of time. We often think of time as something that lasts forever, but it's eternal in a cosmic sense, not in your individual experience."

"A year after your birth, you celebrate your first birthday which is a milestone that marks the passage of time. But imagine if time were running backwards for everyone. Picture this: from the moment a child is born, a timer is attached to them, counting down from seventy-five years. Instead of counting up from zero, the timer counts down from seventy-five to zero. Although the clock would stop once it reaches zero, the concept is intriguing. It suggests that rather than moving forward through time, we are gradually moving towards an end, making each moment all the more precious."

Now, envision yourself in a dark room with nothing but a digital clock on the wall, its red numbers glowing faintly. The timer starts at 15:00 minutes and begins counting down immediately to 14:59. What would you do in this situation?

Your initial reaction would likely be panic. The ticking clock implies a looming danger; as the minutes decrease, the threat of something bad happening grows more real. With a sense of urgency, you would scramble to find a way out. You might search the room desperately for a key, a tool, or any clue that could help you escape before time runs out.

However, consider an alternative scenario where you're placed in the same dark room, but this time, there is no visible clock. After sitting quietly for a while, the digital clock suddenly turns on and begins counting up from 0:00. What would be your response now?

Initially, you might feel a sense of panic, fearing that something dangerous could happen. But as you remain unharmed and the clock continues to count up, you might begin to relax. If you don't perceive an immediate threat and notice that nothing adverse is happening, you might decide to wait for someone to come and let you out or even call for help.

Why does your reaction change so dramatically between the two scenarios? In the first situation, the countdown creates a sense of urgency. Knowing you have only fifteen minutes before something potentially harmful might occur pushes you to act decisively. You realize that time is limited and that you must use every second to escape.

In the second scenario, where time starts from zero and counts up, you initially panic but might eventually believe that there is no immediate danger. Without the pressure of a countdown, you might become complacent, waiting for help rather than trying to escape. The lack of a visible deadline can make you underestimate the urgency of the situation, leading you to miss the opportunity to act and escape in time.

This illustrates a crucial lesson about life: perceiving time as limited can drive you to make the most of every moment. When faced with a clear deadline, you're more likely to act with urgency and determination. Without such a sense of urgency, you might squander valuable opportunities, failing to realize that time is slipping away until it's too late.

"I've never fully realized this before and always thought I had more time than I actually did. It could be happening to you as well."

"It's happening to me, Grandpa!" I admitted. "I already regret it so much. It would be amazing if we could purchase time just like we buy watches. Imagine being able to buy extra hours, 'I need five more hours today, so my day would be twenty-nine hours instead of twenty-four.' What do you think about that?"

My grandpa chuckled and said, "You're neither a complete smart not a dumb. The idea of buying time might sound appealing, but it's important to remember that no matter how much time you think you have, the real challenge is making the most of what you've got."

He continued, "You're also missing something crucial here. Time is constant for everyone, each day is twenty-four hours long, no matter where you are. The sun rises and sets on a schedule that governs everyone's day and night. Nature operates within these fixed time frames, and no matter how you measure your own hours, the total span of life remains unchanged. Trying to quantify your time differently only makes you feel more disconnected and insignificant. Ultimately, someone's seventy-five years are just as finite as your forty-five years. In the end, we all face the same conclusion that the time is limited. Once you run out of it, you can't bring it back no matter what. It is better to act now to avoid the regret later.

I wish I didn't Regret too much

Feeling regretful is a painful experience. As I reach the end of my life, the weight of that regret intensifies. I feel helpless, wishing I could go back in time and alter my choices to avoid this regret. But that's precisely the nature of regret, it can't be changed, and that's what makes it so agonizing.

Regret, in its essence, is uncomfortable, but imagine a life without any regrets - a perfect existence, free from mistakes. It sounds ideal, but perfection is not static; it is a result of growth and learning over time. Imagine acting without any benchmark to measure against. If the first attempt is deemed perfect, it lacks the satisfaction that comes from improvement. True perfection is achieved through effort, skill, and most importantly, learning from mistakes. Mistakes lead to regrets, and those regrets are vital. They allow us to reflect on our errors, learn, and strive not to repeat them. Thus, a life without regrets might seem perfect on the surface, but it would lack depth and the valuable lessons that come from embracing and overcoming our imperfections.

"So, regrets aren't that bad, are they, Grandpa?" I asked.

"They are bad," he replied. "Regrets are troublesome when you don't address them promptly, when you don't take action before it's too late. I understand you're relieved to hear that having regrets is normal, especially since you have some of your own. But instead of using that negative feeling as motivation to make things right, it seems easier to convince yourself that it's okay to feel this way because everyone experiences it. The truth is, acknowledging and confronting your regrets is crucial if you want to learn from them and grow. Ignoring them or pretending they don't matter only delays the possibility of real change."

Regret is a sign, a signal not to dwell on what's already happened, but to learn from it and avoid repeating the same mistakes. It's a form of tough love, coming to you with the intention of guiding you away from past errors. Yet, all too often, we keep calling it back, allowing it to linger.

The experience of regret comes in various stages and intensities, accompanied by a range of emotions. It's not just a single feeling but a complex process, unfolding through multiple stages of reflection and insight.

Mistake: An action taken that shouldn't have been done, though not necessarily an outright prohibition.

Immediate Reaction: The initial emotional response to the mistake, it could be an embarrassment, sadness, shock, grief, etc.

Acknowledged stage: The acceptance that a mistake was made, accompanied by an uncomfortable realization of its consequences.

Lingering stage: A diminished version of the initial regret, still present but less intense.

Amplified stage: A more intense form of regret than 2 but less so than the original, often because no steps were taken to address or rectify the mistake.

Occasional stage: A subdued form of regret, serving as a distant reminder of the original mistake.

Minimal stage: Exists in the background, with minimal emotional impact, as time has softened its sting.

Faded stage: The regret fades from active memory.

Irreversible stage (The Highest Form): A potent form of regret that surfaces when it is too late to make amends, often accompanied by a profound sense of loss or missed opportunity.

Stage	Description
Initial action/Mistake	Actions taken that are regrettable, leading to sense of wrong doing.
Immediate reaction	Initial emotional reactions such as embarrassment, sadness, shock, or grief.
Acknowledged Regret	Recognition and acceptance of the mistake, accompanied by discomfort
Lingering Regret	Persistent sense of regret, though less intense than initial acknowledgement.
Amplified Regret	Intensified regret due to missed opportunities or failure to take corrective action.
Occasional Reminders	Infrequent but poignant reminders of past regrets, prompting introspection.
Minimal Impact	Awareness of a past mistake without significant emotional

	attachment.
Faded Regret	Regret that diminishes over time, no longer actively felt or remembered.
Irreversible Regret	Profound regret where it feels too late to amend or rectify the consequences of the mistake.

Amplified Regret is the stage where regret becomes intensified due to missed opportunities or failure to correct mistakes. At this point, the impact of the mistake is felt strongly enough to drive you to take action, allowing you to mitigate or avoid further regret.

During this stage, you likely have a clear understanding of what went wrong and what steps could potentially rectify or prevent the situation from worsening. It's a crucial moment where prompt action can significantly reduce or even prevent further regret. Acting decisively at this stage can lead to a sense of resolution and diminish the lingering effects of regret.

Therefore, if you find yourself in the Amplified Regret stage, it's wise to act swiftly to address the underlying issues and make decisions that align with your goals and values, thereby minimizing future regrets.

Regrets serve a purpose. They highlight areas for growth. Ignoring them can worsen their impact

In life, it's sometimes crucial to be both discerning and judicious to make the best choices. There was a kid in my neighborhood whom I would occasionally see and wink at. He was undoubtedly a mischievous child, often seen with his mother chasing him around with a stick in hand.

I eventually learned that he was known for his thieving ways in the town. He delighted in stealing pencils, snacks, and toys from homes and shops in the neighborhood. People would often confront his mother, complaining about the losses they had suffered due to his thefts, and they would ask her to compensate for the small but frequent damages.

After receiving numerous scolding from his parents, particularly his mother, he was somewhat under control but still couldn't resist the temptation whenever an opportunity presented itself. One day, as I passed by him, the cheerful boy was whistling and humming a tune. I stopped him and asked, "Aren't you the one who keeps stealing things?" He responded honestly, "No, I stopped stealing. I don't even remember taking anything of yours."

Curious about how such a small kid could manage to steal, I let my curiosity take over and asked him, "How do you even steal? Can you show me how it's done?"

"Do you also like stealing things like me?" he asked with excitement.

I replied, "No, I just want to learn how you do it. I've never stolen anything."

"Okay! Come with me," he said, leading me to a narrow street crowded with shops and people. "Keep watching, and I'll show you how it's done."

He approached one of the shops on the busy street and swiftly stole an apple from the fruit store. Turning to me, he said, "This store doesn't have anyone watching the gate, so the fruit is easy to steal here. You don't need to be afraid at all."

"Now, follow me. Look over there! An ice cream shop. There's usually a boy keeping an eye on the ice creams in the display counter. You have to be very quick to steal one from here. I'll show you," he said.

He went into the shop and, with practiced ease, sneaked open the unlocked refrigerator and grabbed an ice cream while the boy's attention was diverted.

I asked, "What if the boy sees you?"

He replied confidently, "He won't see me. Even if he does, it's just one ice cream. They'd just shout at me, and I'd put it back in the fridge and run away."

After enjoying his ice cream and apple, he asked me to follow him again. This time, he led me to a fancy chocolate shop.

"Look! The shopkeeper is often busy at the counter, so I can sneak in and take some chocolates," he explained.

He waited outside until a queue formed at the billing counter, which drew the shopkeeper's attention. The boy then slipped inside, and I watched as he carefully selected and stole a tiny chocolate from a large box before quickly running out of the shop.

I asked him, "There was a big queue at the counter. You could have easily stolen a whole box of chocolates. Why did you take so long just to steal one small piece?" forgetting I was leading him to wrong paths.

He replied, "It's because if I get caught, the owner won't let me go until he makes me clean the entire shop. It happened once before, and I didn't want to risk it."

"That's okay," he said. "Let's go to one final shop." He dragged me to an adjacent store. "This is a famous toy shop in town. I rarely steal here because it's easy to get caught, there are cameras and workers at every row."

He went inside, picked up a toy, and started to run outside. Just as he was about to escape, one of the shopkeepers caught him, gave him a sharp knock on the head, snatched the toy from his hand, and kicked him out of the store.

The kid rubbed his head and said, "That's very painful!"

"It's okay," He consoled himself and continued, "Let's check out one last shop."

He led me to a shop and said, "I never steal from here. Once, when I tried, the owner complained to my mother and beat me up badly. I never told my mother about it."

"So, you don't steal from here anymore?" I asked.

"Yes, I don't," he replied. "But this one looks like the easiest shop for you. The owner is sleeping inside, and there's nobody watching."

But, I said, "Do you want to give a try?"

"Nope. Not worth it," he said with a wave. "Bye!" And with that, he left.

That day, the kid taught me invaluable lessons about regret: some regrets are worth experiencing, while others are not. He was wise to choose his battles considering how to act when caught, how to avoid the heavy burden of regret from stealing, and how to embrace the lighter, sillier regrets. He understood that not every regret serves as a life lesson, nor is every choice devoid of value. We should all strive to be like that kid, making thoughtful decisions and choosing our regrets wisely. But not develop his stealing skills. His every mistake had a regret attached to it, but he chose to say "It's ok" for the most and "I don't want to do it again" for few. You must be smart enough to learn this and not dwell on every regret.

For example, If you choose to study instead of going out with friends, but end up going out, playing hard, sharing laughter, and making memories, the regret isn't very heavy; the pleasure here outweighs the guilt. It might have been better to stick to your plans and study, but the joy of spending time with friends can be more rewarding. However, if this becomes a frequent pattern, remember the kid's advice from the final shop: "Not worth it." In such cases, the pleasure may not justify the regret.

Be a smart judge of your choices, opt for the difficult path when the guilt outweighs the pleasure. When pleasure outweighs the guilt, which is rare, allowing for some regret can be worth it. Choose wisely, balancing your decisions between long-term goals and immediate satisfaction.

Some regrets come as blessings, offering opportunities for growth. If you ignore them and let them fade, they often return stronger, manifesting as deeper regrets that prevent you from benefiting from them, which is why they can hurt the most.

On the other hand, some regrets are inconsequential. While they are genuine feelings, it's okay to experience them from time to time. Regret is rarely a solitary emotion; it often comes bundled with guilt, frustration, anger, sadness, and more. It's a complex mix of emotions tied to something you did or that happened to you.

So, sometimes, regrets are simply part of life. You don't have to let them overwhelm you or paralyze you into inaction. Life can be tough, and when it is, it's important to remember that some things are beyond your control. Accept the setbacks, acknowledge the emotions, but don't let them prevent you from moving forward. Sometimes, things just happen, and all you can do is take them as they come.

At the same time, once you understand how regrets work, you might start viewing even minor regrets as major offenses. Don't fall into that trap. We are all human, prone to making mistakes, and sometimes we don't perform at our best. We might mess up, either knowingly or unknowingly, and that's perfectly okay. Accept it and move on, don't dwell on it.

For instance, if you could have performed better in an interview but stumbled on a question or forgot an answer, that's fine. Humans forget things and make mistakes. Acknowledge the error, learn from it, and use it as a challenge for next time. Don't let it consume your time and energy by replaying it over and over for days, weeks, or months.

Similarly, if you were at a party and saw someone you found attractive but didn't approach them, that's also okay. You might regret not taking the chance, but don't let it overshadow your experience or your self-worth. Life is full of opportunities and moments that pass us by, and it's natural to have regrets. Accept them, learn from them, and move forward and approach them next time.

"Wow, Grandpa, you're using examples to relate it to me," I thought, feeling a surge of enthusiasm as I listened more intently.

"I know you'll pay closer attention now," he said with a knowing smile, and continued with his story.

"Imagine there was a beautiful girl at the party, and you decided to approach her. Instead of saying, 'Hey, you look beautiful. Would you like to join me for a coffee?' you ended up saying, 'Hey, you look like a coffee. How beautiful is that?' You'd likely feel embarrassed afterward. That's okay. You were captivated by her, and sometimes things just don't come out as intended.

The key is to learn from the experience and move on quickly. Don't let it ruin the rest of your time at the party by dwelling on it."

So, you're saying it's okay to mess up and feel regretful?

"Yes, sometimes". He replied.

I often regret regretting too much. For example, I knew about a stock that was poised to skyrocket but didn't purchase it. Instead of focusing on the profits I did make from other shares, I chose to dwell on the missed opportunity. I let myself cry over what I didn't have rather than appreciating and enjoying the success I had already achieved. It's easy to get caught up in what could have been, but it's important to recognize and be grateful for the moments and achievements that bring us happiness.

Asking yourself, "What do I have?" can lead to either gratitude or sorrow, depending on how you choose to frame it.

The perspective you adopt will shape your emotional response. Decide in advance how you want to feel about that moment and let that choice guide your outlook. By focusing on what you have and the positives in your life, you can cultivate gratitude and find contentment, rather than letting sorrow take over.

There were two kids from the slums of Mumbai, born into the poorest families and destined to lead a life of hardship unless a miracle occurred, either within or beyond their circumstances.

Each day, they would wake up and head out to beg on the streets. Their daily routine was simple: find people who might give them some cash. Every morning, the two kids walked together until they reached the edge of their slum, at which point they would part ways and follow different paths.

One of the kids would head to the left side of the slum, where the path led to a busy town area filled with hotels and street stores. The streets were always crowded and lively. To navigate through the heat and the throngs of people, the kid would push through the crowd and begin asking for money from strangers. He would often say he hadn't eaten for a long time or sometimes request money to help feed his family.

Occasionally, people would give him some cash, and sometimes the hotels would provide him with food.

On the other hand, the other kid went to the wealthier side of the city, where tall buildings and multi-cuisine restaurants dominated the landscape. The roads here were generally less crowded and frequented by wealthy individuals and lavish cars. Although there were fewer people, those who did donate often gave larger sums of money. Additionally, when the kid stood outside the restaurants, customers leaving the restaurants would sometimes hand him leftover tasty food in take-away containers.

At the end of the day, the two kids would return to their slum and sit together, sharing their experiences.

The kid who went to the town area excitedly told the other, "I had a good day today. It was really sunny, but the streets were crowded, and I managed to find some shade under the shop blinds. There were thousands of people shopping, and a few of them gave me some money, which added up to a decent amount. I even got some food from one of the hotels. It wasn't the best, but it was better than starving. I hope things stay like this, and I'll be happy. How was your day?"

The other kid, feeling disheartened, replied, "There's nothing great about begging on the streets. The rich people live such luxurious lives, the cars they ride in move so fast, and the restaurants and hotels they go to are enormous. The shopping malls are all shiny, and I wasn't even allowed to enter them. The rich kids eat whatever they want, are dressed so nicely, and smell good. They're clean and tidy, and most of them wear jewelry and watches that we can only dream of. My day was really bad."

"That's okay," said the first kid. "Didn't they even give you any money? You can come with me tomorrow," he suggested.

The other kid replied, "No, they did give me cash. Only three people gave me money, but look at these notes." He showed the large denominations he had received from just those three people.

"This is a lot! I never get any notes on my side of the streets, only coins," said the other kid. "So, what are you still unhappy about?"

"I don't know," the other kid said. "Seeing those people, I was just struck by how far apart our lives are. They gave me cash and even offered me some tasty food, but it's not the life I want. I want to live like them, not beg on the streets."

The first kid replied, "You must be joking. That's not how it is. I'm actually glad with how my day went. See you tomorrow. I'm going to sleep now; I'm very tired." With that, he waved goodbye.

You must now decide which kid you want to be. Do you want to adopt the perspective of the kid who was content with what he had, appreciating the small victories and what he received each day, or the perspective of the kid who felt disheartened and found regret at every stage by recognizing what he was missing, focusing on the gap between his life and the lives of the wealthy, and overlooking the value of what he already had? The choice is yours: to embrace gratitude for what you have or to dwell on what you don't, missing the opportunity to recognize and appreciate your own achievements and blessings.

"That's a great question, Grandpa! I don't have the right answer," I replied.

My grandpa smiled and said, "Wear the perspective sunglasses that suit you best for that moment. If you're too focused on being content with what you have, you might miss out on opportunities for growth and improvement. Conversely, if you're too focused on what you don't have, you risk wasting the present by not appreciating and making the most of what you already possess."

Be happy, but don't be satisfied. Aim for more and work towards it. Regrets are short-lived with consistent action; they become lasting when you stop thinking big and face them at the end.

"There's also the option to be satisfied, isn't there, Grandpa? What if the kid who was happy with what he had on the crowded streets was also satisfied? Isn't that the ideal state of mind?" I asked curiously.

"Yes, it sounds ideal," Grandpa replied. "But that doesn't last forever for this kid. If he's only happy and satisfied, he might not take steps to improve his situation, save money, or plan for the future. If the streets become less crowded, if prices rise, or if hotel owners stop giving him food, he could quickly lose both his happiness and satisfaction. Without preparation or growth, his life could become very difficult."

Satisfaction is often misunderstood. It's not just a feeling within; it's shaped by external factors that influence your life, food, shelter, home, belongings, family, money, and relationships. It's not a detached, internal state. True satisfaction comes from having an abundance of these elements, not just for today but ideally for the foreseeable future. Don't believe in those godly proclaimed people telling your satisfaction must come within you. Even having a little more than what you need for a few days can create a sense of abundance and satisfaction.

Chase Abundance.

"So, the other kid was aware of this but wasn't satisfied or happy. That's worse than losing both on the same day. He had reasons to be happy but chose not to, while he found many reasons to be sad. So, who's the ideal kid, Grandpa?" I asked.

Grandpa replied, "The ideal kid is the one who explored both worlds, the rich streets and the crowded areas. He finds joy and appreciation in what he has, even when he feels he lacks something. When he's in the rich streets and feels he has nothing, he goes to the crowded streets and realizes how fortunate he was to get that cash and food. Then, he returns to the rich streets, seeking new opportunities and reasons to improve his situation. This kid balances gratitude and ambition, always striving for growth while appreciating what he has."

He was happy with what he had while also recognizing what he still needed to achieve and working towards it. Even when he couldn't reach his goals, he remained grateful for what he had.

Don't waste today worrying about yesterday or tomorrow. Use today wisely, learn from the past, plan for the future, and make the most of the present moment.

"Listen, kid, regret can be very deceiving. Sometimes you feel it when you don't need to, and other times you don't feel it when you should. Experiencing either or both can stall your progress in life. Regretting when you don't need to is worse than not regretting when you should. In the former case, you're emotionally overwhelmed and caught up in your feelings. In the latter, you'll simply face the consequences in due time."

"So, it's more important to know what not to regret than what to regret. They might seem similar, but they're as different as a monkey finding a banana, peeling it, eating the fruit, and throwing the peel away, while a beetle coming along and starts chewing on the discarded peel. You need to choose whether you want to be like the monkey, focusing on the valuable fruit, or like the beetle, fixating on what's left behind."

"I'd prefer to be a monkey, Grandpa! It eat the fruit."

"You already are one," he smiled.

I asked, "How can regretting too much affect us?"

He replied, **"Regretting too much, or dwelling on things that don't necessarily need regret, will just lead you into an infinite loop of being regretful."**

Imagine a kid who's been told not to cry when it's time to go to school. As the school bus arrives, he starts crying. To stop him, his mom scolds him, but he continues to cry. Frustrated, she slaps him, and he only cries harder. His dad hears the commotion, comes over, and slaps him again, but the crying intensifies. Despite further attempts to stop him, each slap only makes him cry more and more.

Just as one lie can lead to many others, one unnecessary regret can spiral into countless regrets, endlessly compounding. **Regret serves to help us avoid repeating past mistakes, not to change what's already happened.** No human or living being can travel through time to alter the past or the future. Therefore, the purpose of regret is to learn and improve, not to dwell endlessly on what cannot be changed. Excessive regret only erodes the present, which will eventually become the past and lead to even more regret.

Sometimes, it's worth laughing at a few regrets. Not every moment is about correction or learning; some are just amusing memories in their own right.

I remember a particularly memorable moment from my graduation. I had volunteered to give a speech welcoming the chief guest at our annual day celebrations. On the big day, I was prepared and eager, but as I climbed onto the stage, my friends who were seated closer to the front started cheering loudly and trying to distract me.

Despite my efforts to stay focused on my speech, my friends' antics made it difficult. I pressed on, introducing the guest and talking about his achievements, but their cheers grew louder and more distracting. In a moment of frustration, I shouted, "Hey! Shut up!" forgetting I was holding a microphone. The amplification of my outburst startled the chief guest, causing him to lose his balance and fall down the stairs. The audience erupted in laughter.

Panicked, I rushed to help him back up and quickly apologized. I couldn't continue my speech, and I was mortified by the chaos and my loss of composure. I was also furious with my friends and decided I would confront them after the event.

When the event concluded, I marched over to where my friends were sitting near the cafeteria, ready to scold them. But as soon as I approached, the atmosphere turned quiet, and they all looked at me with apprehension. Just as I was about to speak, one friend burst out laughing, and soon, they were all laughing hysterically. I couldn't help but join in.

We reminisced about the chief guest's reaction and the whole scene, and though it wasn't right to laugh at someone's fear or mishap, the situation was so absurd that we found it funny. If I had stayed angry and held onto my regret of not performing my duty right, I would have missed out on this joyful, bonding moment.

In the end, it was a funny and unforgettable experience with my friends, one we still laugh about every time we meet. It was okay to have messed up; it wasn't that serious in the grand scheme of things. I realized that if I had let my regret overshadow the laughter and camaraderie, I would have missed out on a cherished memory.

I remember another incident from my school days. During Holi, a festival where people throw colors at each other, I decided not to step outside because I knew my friends would make a mess with me and my clothes. So, I decided to stay locked inside the house and avoid going out that day.

I woke up early that morning, took a bath, prayed, and put on a new shirt my father had bought for me. I asked my mother not to open the door if anyone knocked and, even if she did, to tell my friends that I wasn't home. Dressed up and settled inside, I tried to relax and enjoy the holiday. After a while, I heard a knock on the door. Meanwhile, my mother was busy in the kitchen cooking delicious sweets for the family.

As soon as I heard the knock, I called my mom to check who it was. Since she was busy cooking, she asked me to check myself. Afraid to open the door but unable to ignore the persistent knocks, I hesitated. My mother then shouted, "Open the damn door! It might be someone wanting to see your father."

Reluctantly, I opened the door, only to be met with a splash of colors all over my face and new shirt. It was my friends. I regretted opening the door instantly, feeling sad and disappointed with myself. Unable to say a word, I simply closed the door in sorrow and went inside to change my clothes.

My mother asked me what had happened. I shouted in frustration, "It's all because of you!" I was consumed with regret for opening the door. I hated myself for it and felt like a loser, as if I had been cheated.

I didn't speak to anyone for the rest of the day. My beautiful holiday was overshadowed by my regret, as I dwelled on the ruined new shirt and felt sorry for myself all day.

The next day, I went to school still feeling sad and disappointed. As soon as I entered the classroom, I noticed that all my friends had light shades of color on their faces from the previous day. Everyone, except me, still had traces of the colors on their hands and faces.

As I began to sit down, I heard whispers about the fun they'd had. It turned out that everyone in my class had joined in the celebrations, getting drenched in colors and water. Many of their new shirts were stained as well. Despite their initial reluctance to open the door, they laughed about how they had failed and enjoyed the experience instead of regretting it too much.

I asked one of my friends if he had regretted opening the door like I did. He replied, "I did at first, but as soon as I started putting colors on everyone's faces, it felt amazing and fun. I regretted opening the door only briefly. Once I joined in, I completely forgot about it. We had a great time. Honestly, I would have regretted it more if I had stayed inside and been sad like you did."

That hit me hard. I realized I wasn't the only one who had been disappointed by failing my plan and staying home for the rest of the day. While I had wallowed in my regret, all my friends had turned their regret into an opportunity for fun.

That was the day I learned not to replay hurtful scenarios over and over in my head. Sometimes, you have to laugh at yourself, move forward, and embrace what life throws at you.

I realized that while I thought my holiday was wasted because my plan had failed, my friends actually had a better time than they had planned. They didn't let their regret hold them back.

If your plan fails, don't regret it so much that you miss out on a better opportunity that comes your way.

My grandpa, asked which regrets are worth regretting. I replied that it depends on the situation and how much time has passed, though I wasn't entirely sure.

He explained "No regret should be regretted. Even if you experience regret, whether it's valid or not, don't let yourself regret the regret itself. Accept that regrets are part of the process. If the regret is valid, learn from it and move on. If it's not valid, let it go without letting it affect you. The key is to not dwell on regrets, regardless of whether they are justified or not."

Steps for Productive Action and Reflection

Take Action: Step forward with your decision.

Assess Outcomes: Your action may lead to regret, or it may not.

Evaluate Regret: If regret arises, take time to validate it.

Determine Validity:

- o **Invalid Regret:** If the regret doesn't outweigh the mistake or stems from overthinking, recognize it as invalid.

- o **Valid Regret:** If the regret is based on a genuine misstep that had significant consequences or missed opportunities, acknowledge it as valid.

Let Go of Invalid Regret: Don't dwell on feelings that are unproductive.

Embrace Valid Regret: If the regret is valid, use it as a chance for growth and correction. Move forward instead of lingering in regret.

Learn and Act Again: After gaining insights, take another action, and continue the cycle.

I wish I took care of my Health.

My grandpa asked me if I knew any quote related to health. I replied, "Health is wealth," since that's the only one that came to mind.

"I've asked this question to over a hundred people, and ninety-eight of them gave the same answer." Grandpa continued, "Everyone knows 'health is wealth,' but they don't always act on it. Their idea of wealth is different. If everyone pursued health as if it were the only kind of wealth, people would be happier and more united."

There's a sequence of priorities you need to follow to make your life meaningful, Grandpa said. "First comes wealth, then family, followed by money, purpose, and finally, happiness."

"What's the difference between wealth and money, Grandpa? Aren't they the same?" I asked, puzzled. He looked at me with a hint of disappointment and replied, "What was the quote you just mentioned?"

"What's money without health?" Grandpa continued; I regret not pursuing that healthy wealth in my life. The regret is even stronger because I knew I should have done it, but I failed to.

Most of us fail at this, neglecting our health and not striving for a healthy body and mind. The universe is so complex, with millions of living species, each functioning in different ways. Yet, human life is uniquely precious, vulnerable, and beautifully mysterious. Our advances in science and technology, and the incredible progress in medical sciences allows doctors to understand and treat what's happening within our bodies, doesn't that sound brilliant?

"It does sound brilliant. But if you trust science and doctors so much, why aren't you confident about the surgery scheduled for you?" I asked.

"That's different," he replied, clearly annoyed.

"Alright," I said, and continued listening.

Despite advancements in technology and our understanding of the human body, many mysteries remain unsolved. Few diseases are still incurable, and once the human body is declared dead, it cannot be revived. Death is such a profound mystery. A living, talking, sensing body becomes an immovable entity after death, and it is beyond human comprehension. No one on this planet can bring the dead back to life.

Even with riches aplenty, when facing the final hours, neither wealth nor technology can rescue you, only your own health and well-being prevail.

There was a millionaire who inherited his wealth rather than earning it through hard work. If he had, he might not have been so obese. His pride in his money meant he never experienced true hunger; his stomach was always full, just like his bank account. With luxuries at his beck and call and people to handle every task around his mansion, he had nothing to do but eat, sleep, and pass the time.

He would buy everything he could dream of or want, yet he lacked a sense of achievement because the things were bought, not earned. He believed he could buy everything, including health. When the doctor visited his mansion for the first time because the millionaire complained of a heartache, the doctor advised him to exercise and limit his food intake.

The millionaire, furious, replied, "How dare you tell me what I should do and eat? What do you own to dictate my life? How many millions do you have?"

The doctor, recognizing the man's behavior, calmly said, "I'll see you at the hospital when the time comes."

The millionaire continued to believe that his money could protect him from everything. When the heartache returned with greater intensity, he was rushed to the hospital. There, the same non-millionaire doctor examined him and confirmed it was a heart attack. The doctor instructed the millionaire to wear a surgical mask, stop eating for next few hours, take the prescribed medicines, and undergo various tests.

The millionaire now obeyed every command, like a child being directed by a mother.

The doctor examined him thoroughly and concluded that no amount of money could prevent the millionaire from passing away. Desperate, the millionaire begged and promised his entire fortune to the doctor, but it was to no avail. The doctor could not revive him from his deathbed. All the cash in the bank remained untouched as the millionaire was buried deep in the ground, his skin and bones eventually disappeared.

Nature itself is a stunning creation, its origins unknown yet profoundly believable. It offers everything, the good and the bad, and sometimes these are deceptive, reflecting the complexity of the cosmos.

Take food, for example. Something that tastes heavenly, like a buttery, deep-fried dish loaded with cheese and spices, can block your arteries and harm your health. On the other hand, a vegetable or fruit, though it may taste less exciting and lacks all the indulgent extras, will help keep your body healthy.

"Why is the universe set up this way?" I asked curiously.

If something feels good to us, like tasty food, why does it often lead to a bad reaction, like poor health? And when something isn't as enjoyable, like bland vegetables, why does it result in something good, like better health? I've always wondered about this but never found a profound answer.

Grandpa nodded thoughtfully and replied, "It's a question that has puzzled many. The balance between pleasure and consequence often reflects a deeper truth about nature and the universe."

"It's about the value," Grandpa explained. "Value is defined by the effort you put into something. If eating fries and burgers all day could make you fit and healthy, or if every tasty food led to a sharp and strong physique, everyone would be healthy and fit. But that's not the case. The true value comes when something is desired by many but achieved by only a few through hard work. It's the effort and struggle that give value to what we attain."

"Eating bitter things is tough but rewarding," Grandpa continued. "It's called a reward not because of the action itself but because of the result. The action is never rewarding in itself; if it were, the result wouldn't be considered a reward."

"When you work hard at the gym, you endure pain, but you feel good, thanks to the endorphins released. You'll feel even better when you lose weight and become fit. The action of working out itself isn't rewarding; that's why it's tough. If the action were rewarding, everyone would do it. The true reward comes from the results, which are achieved through suffering. That's what makes it valuable."

"Reward comes after suffering. That's why it's called a reward. If it came before the suffering, it wouldn't be a reward, it would be suffering in disguise."

There was a scientist born in the 1920s who was incredibly enthusiastic about technology. He spent most of his days in the laboratory and library, experimenting and reading about scientific advancements. His love for the field knew no bounds, and he would get excited about any news or new inventions related to science.

But he soon realized that he was mortal and wouldn't be alive forever to witness future advancements. Unable to accept this, he sought ways to achieve immortality. He delved into many books, consulted professors and doctors, and explored human life and the concept of immortality. He even studied holy scripts from various religions and cultures that depicted immortal beings, searching for any possible method he could replicate to attain immortality himself.

Alas, nothing worked. He wasn't godly; he was a normal human being with a limited lifespan on this planet. No matter how knowledgeable, rich, kind, or accomplished he might be, he would eventually have to take his last breath.

However, his hopes didn't diminish. After speaking to many doctors and professors, he came to understand that, for him, immortality meant living the longest possible life. It meant surpassing the average human lifespan, breaking existing records, and witnessing at least one great innovation before his death.

For that, he realized the only way was to be as healthy as possible. His goal became to be the healthiest human being ever known, aiming to outlive expectations and fulfill his wish.

He tried everything to become healthier, eating a good diet, exercising, managing stress, running, avoiding unhealthy foods, grooming himself, and maintaining a healthy lifestyle. Gradually, he began to feel better and healthier.

In the past, while immersed in his work in the laboratory, he hadn't paid much attention to what he ate, how many hours he slept, or how often he exercised. None of these aspects had been acknowledged or prioritized.

But now, it was the opposite. He was acutely aware of what was good for him and what wasn't. He knew when to sleep, what to eat, and what to avoid.

He adhered to this new way of life. As he became healthier physically, his mental well-being improved as well. Gradually, he became calmer and more pleasant. His passion for technology remained, but it no longer consumed him. Although he still wished to live long, he had come to accept the possibility of leaving this world. His journey toward one destination revealed multiple new paths and opportunities.

Nevertheless, the man lived to be a hundred years old. His contributions to science and his quest for immortality became so renowned that he was interviewed in his final days. He answered to the questions asked as:

Q: "Your profound love for technology has contributed to your living for 100 years. How do you feel about it?"

A: "Accomplished. It didn't take me long to realize that we are mortals and that chasing immortality is both insane and humanly impossible."

Q: "Does that mean you should live life as you want and just accept death when it comes?"

A: "Death affects not the one who is dying, but those are left behind. I'd say, live a long life and make your loved ones happy. While you can't achieve immortality, you can be healthy and enjoy a long life."

Q: "What recent advancements in technology have you found groundbreaking?"

A: "AI. I never imagined automation and artificial intelligence would advance so much and have such a profound impact on human life. Also, electric cars have impressed me greatly. I feel accomplished to have witnessed these developments and am curious about what the future holds for the next generations."

Q: "Why do you think people should aim for a healthy life?"

A: "Because it's everything. Living life to the fullest doesn't mean doing extravagant things but using your abilities to the best in everyday activities. A healthy body and mind help you accomplish everything you want. For instance, if you're playing a sport, would you prefer being able to run fast, jump, and enjoy the game, or being unable to participate and left out? Health isn't just physical; being physically healthy also supports mental well-being too."

Q: "What would you say to people who don't want to live as long as you did?"

A: "Good. If that's how they feel, then they should die sooner."

Q: "What do you think about people who don't believe in being healthy and choose to live fully, even if it means a shorter life?"

A: "Great. Do what works for you. But if death comes sooner due to health complications, it's an incomplete life. Your loved ones will miss you and wish they could have you back, but you won't be there. A healthy life isn't just about longevity; it's about the quality of life. You could live healthily and still face unexpected accidents, but if you're fortunate and avoid such risks, the additional time is a bonus. I'm living proof of both quality and quantity in life. Aim for that balance; otherwise, you might regret it just before you're gone."

Q: "What would you say to motivate people to lead a healthy life?"

A: "Motivation is a cheat code. It doesn't always work. For a healthy life, you should focus on discipline instead. Motivation comes and goes; it's the feeling of wanting to do something, sometimes. Discipline is about doing it regardless of how you feel. Motivation might help occasionally, but discipline works all the time. If someone is unhealthy, they will understand how it feels and will likely find their own reasons to commit to a healthier lifestyle without needing external motivation."

Imagine a fit man who is neither obese nor lacking in endurance. He feels great when walking, his breath is controlled, his body doesn't feel heavy, his steps are steady. He can easily bend to tie his laces, jump over puddles, roll if needed, and run to catch a thief who steals his wallet.

Now, consider an unhealthy man. He feels his weight with every step, his breath is heavy, and his steps are unsteady. He needs frequent rests, cannot run, bend, jump, or roll. If someone steals from him, all he can do is give up and scream.

As I mentioned, health isn't just about physical appearance. The healthier man returns home without feeling exhausted. He can read a book, meditate, exercise, take a bath, laugh heartily, avoid stress, smile frequently, speak kindly, attract positive attention, and enjoy the company of friends. He feels fulfilled before bed and sleeps soundly.

In contrast, the unhealthy man feels disappointed, tired, regretful, and lacks confidence. He has ambitious goals, much like the healthier man, but struggles to achieve them because he hasn't disciplined his body, which in turn affects his mind. Now, consider if you really need motivation, or if discipline and a healthy lifestyle might be what you truly need.

People who aim health are disinclined rather than motivated. They suffer the pain of it to avoid the pain of regret.

His interview went viral on the internet, and the old man, who had lived to be 100 years, passed away peacefully in his sleep while watching a TV show titled The Tech 2224, which explored how the world might look 200 years from then.

Sometimes, being disciplined is crucial for living a longer and healthier life, not just for yourself but for others as well. Imagine the grief of losing a loved one. Their departure leaves a void that can never truly be filled. I lost my brother to cancer, a friend to liver disease, and another friend's father to a heart attack. All of them left us far too soon.

Their sudden departures left a profound impact. I still feel the void my brother's absence has created, and his wife continues to miss him every day. My friend still struggles with the loss of his father, and it took him a long time to come to terms with the trauma. If they had taken better care of their health and lived longer, they could have made a significant difference in the lives of those around them.

Here I am, lying in bed suffering from cancer, and I regret not taking better care of my health. There were many opportunities to quit smoking, eat healthier, and get regular checkups before things went wrong. Yet, I chose to live with these regrets until the end.

I know my passing will bring pain to you and the family, but I'm grateful that I was able to be here for 80 years. I feel partially accomplished, having witnessed much of your success and been present for my children's upbringing. The thought of leaving my family while they were still young is unbearable, but at least I can find some solace in knowing I was there for them as they grew.

When I started smoking, my brother and I were enjoying cigars under the cool shade of a coconut tree, unaware that our dad was passing by. As soon as he came into view, my brother quickly threw his cigar away and stood there, frozen. I didn't understand why he reacted that way and kept smoking mine, puzzled by his sudden change in behavior.

I noticed my brother's eyes widen with a look of sheer terror. Curious, I looked to my right and saw our father walking towards us. Fear surged through me, and my entire body screamed at me to run. I did just that, with my brother following suit, despite having already thrown away his cigar.

We escaped and didn't return home until late at night, sneaking in with the hope that our father was asleep. Unfortunately, as we tried to enter the house, we found him waiting for us at the main door, leaving us no choice but to surrender and ask for his forgiveness. Surprisingly, he didn't punish us. Instead, he explained how smoking would damage our health and urged us to quit immediately.

Like many who enjoy smoking, we barely listened. We were young and stubborn, aware of the dangers but unwilling to change. We came up with excuses to justify our habit: life is short, we would die anyway, not everyone who smokes gets cancer, and a hundred more reasons to convince ourselves that quitting wasn't necessary.

The next day, as I walked towards the same coconut tree, I briefly considered taking my father's words seriously and thought about quitting smoking for a healthier lifestyle. But like many others, I succumbed to temptation. I lit up one cigar, then another, and another, and it didn't stop until I was eighty. One of my excuses proved to be true: I smoked for eighty years, but it didn't save me from cancer at eighty, while my brother was taken by the disease at just twenty-seven.

When I was posted to a different city for work, I moved there alone before bringing your grandmother with me. During that time, she always urged me to eat healthily. She understood that cooking at home might be challenging, but she encouraged me to try. She also reminded me not to get consumed by work and to make time for physical activities.

I nodded in agreement like a student in front of a teacher, but I didn't follow any of her advice. I ate out every day, never cooked for myself, continued smoking with friends, stayed buried in work, and never exercised or embraced a healthy lifestyle. After six months in the new city, my poor habits caught up with me. I became seriously ill, and the doctors diagnosed me with a severe digestive condition that required surgery, followed by six months of rest.

During those six months, while a few of my colleagues were getting promoted, moving their families, and enjoying life, I was stuck at home, resting and doing almost nothing. I deeply regret not taking better care of my health back then. When you're surrounded by friends or a group of people who share the same unhealthy habits, it's incredibly challenging to maintain a unique, disciplined routine. No matter how strong your resolve or controlling your mindset, it's almost inevitable to eventually fall into the same patterns as those around you. You find yourself compelled to conform.

When I was with my colleagues, I genuinely wanted to cook healthy meals at home, but they insisted on dining out at restaurants with them. I could decline once, twice, or even three times, but eventually, I was swept along with the group. I started to eat like them, think like them, and behave like them, even though I knew deep down it was wrong. We often tend to adopt negative behaviors when others do them, believing, "If they can do it, so can I." However, we rarely draw motivation from the positive actions of others.

It's crucial to choose your company wisely. This doesn't mean you have to abandon your friends or loved ones just because their lifestyle and habits don't align with yours. Instead, you can seek out a new group that encourages you to improve and grow. You can maintain relationships with your old friends while surrounding yourself with people who inspire you to level up, become a better person, and stay healthy. Being in environments that challenge you to be competitive and strive for better will have a positive impact on your life.

Never settle for relationships or situations that demotivate you, pull you down, or offer a false sense of joy and happiness. As I've mentioned before, true rewards come through enduring and overcoming suffering. You can't alter this fundamental truth by going against the natural order.

I remember when I was in my forties, there was a medical camp in our neighborhood. Everyone decided to get tested to ensure everything was fine with their health. Except for me, nearly everyone took advantage of the discounted tests offered as part of the promotional campaign. I was convinced my body was in good shape and didn't need any tests, so I skipped the opportunity, trying to save even the small amount the promotion offered.

A week later, when the test results came in, three of my neighbors were diagnosed with serious illnesses and promptly began their treatments. Learning about their conditions made me uneasy and I started to worry if I had made a mistake by not getting my own body checked before it was too late. Despite this, I stubbornly stuck to my belief that my body was perfect and continued to ignore the possibility of any underlying issues.

Three months later, another medical camp was held, but this time at higher prices. Persuaded by your grandmother, I decided to pay the increased amount and get the tests done. When the results came back, I was shocked to find that my cholesterol and fat levels were dangerously high. I rushed to the hospital with the reports and consulted a doctor, who informed me that the fat had been accumulating rapidly. If I had gotten tested four months earlier, the issue might have been manageable by now. That day, I deeply regretted not having taken the opportunity to check my health sooner.

Skipping the check-up when it was needed could have spared me from a serious illness. The doctors prescribed six months' worth of medication, which ended up costing me a fortune. The amount I saved with the initial promotional discount was now multiplied tenfold in my current medical expenses.

At every opportunity to get healthier, I avoided taking action. Eventually, I realized this before it was too late and began focusing on improving my health. Exercising, walking, and maintaining a clean diet helped me live a long life. However, as I've mentioned, it's not just about the lifespan but the quality of it. Although I made it to eighty, there were many years where I could have significantly improved the quality of my life had I taken better care of my health earlier.

Sometimes, people will try to correct their mistakes, but not everyone will succeed. The millionaire who died in the hospital had a younger brother who was just like him. When his brother passed away, he realized that no amount of money could save him if he didn't take care of his health. He began trying to become healthier, but as we know, health isn't something you achieve in a day or two, nor is it a destination you reach and then stop. Becoming healthier is a continual practice. Once you're healthy, you must maintain that health; it's an ongoing commitment.

The younger brother struggled to maintain a healthy lifestyle for more than a week and repeatedly failed. Had he persisted a bit longer, he might have crossed the saturation point and gained the momentum needed to achieve his goals, much like in any other human endeavor. Most people give up after a few failures, not realizing that just a little more persistence could lead to success. In many cases, success is only a few attempts away.

The brother came to the realization that he wouldn't make it much longer and would have to face death in a few months. He reached out to renowned scientists around the world, commissioning them to create a chamber that would preserve his body without decomposition after his death. His hope was that, in the future, advancements in technology might enable them to revive him, using the funds he would leave behind for the endeavor.

The scientists informed him that such a task was nearly impossible and there were no guarantees of future advancements that could make it feasible. They also cautioned that, considering inflation and the cost of such experiments, even the substantial sum he intended to leave might not be enough to cover the expenses.

He replied, "I don't know if it will happen, but I remain hopeful. As you mentioned, at least let them consider me as an option for experimentation. Even if the money isn't sufficient, they might still use my preserved body. After all, where else can they find a non-decomposed body from the past?"

The scientists agreed and asked for six months to build the chamber. The brother used all his strength to hold on for those six months, and when the chamber was finally ready, he was overjoyed. The scientists explained the chamber's workings: it was constructed from titanium, resistant to corrosion, with advanced sealing mechanisms, a precise temperature control system, and chemicals like formaldehyde to ensure preservation for hundreds of years. They had invested millions in its creation, aiming to keep his body intact until future advancements might make revival possible.

The brother was elated and filled with anticipation for the future. He left his body with great hope and a smile on his face, just days after the chamber was completed. True to their word, the scientists placed him in the chamber, activated the temperature control, sealed it securely, and stored it safely in an advanced basement beneath the millionaire brother's house.

Regular inspections were carried out every month to ensure the chamber remained intact. During the fifth inspection, a scientist noticed a small but troubling leakage of chemicals. Alarmed, he quickly alerted the other scientists. Upon further investigation, they discovered that the hermetic seal on the chamber had likely failed, allowing moisture and oxygen to seep in. This breach could hasten the decomposition of the body.

The scientists worked urgently to reseal the chamber, hoping to prevent further damage. Despite their best efforts, the seal's failure spread to other parts of the chamber, and within a day, the chamber split into two pieces. The body, once perfectly preserved, began to decompose. The initial signs were subtle, but soon the color changed, the stomach bloated, and the decomposition accelerated beyond their control.

Alas, despite their best efforts, the scientists failed to prevent the decay. The body was eventually buried in the backyard of the mansion, and with it, the millionaire's hope of future resurrection was laid to rest.

All that truly mattered was the time he had while he was alive, not the hope he clung to after his death. He passed away with dreams of revival, yet he would never awaken to see those dreams realized. When he was fully alive and had the chance to pursue a healthier life, he ignored it. How could a lifeless body ever achieve what a living, functioning body could not?

The scientists were deeply upset about their failure. They gathered to discuss how they couldn't preserve the millionaire inside the chamber despite investing millions in its creation.

One scientist reflected, "No matter how much money you have, you can't live happily if you aren't healthy."

Another scientist responded, "Truly said. Even the dead couldn't rest in peace with all that money."

The former scientist continued, "The nature of law is such that it functions autonomously, without intervention, if it isn't disrupted. Consider a physical being: from the moment of birth, the body's systems work seamlessly. The heart pumps, the kidneys filter, the lungs oxygenate, and the nerves transmit signals, all without external commands or interference. It's only when one harms oneself with poor lifestyle choices and harmful activities that these systems begin to deteriorate. The natural laws are exquisitely efficient; no technology or external augmentation can match nature's performance. Artificial means are perpetually uncertain in comparison."

"That proves every human being must strive to make their body and mind function at their best, in harmony with the laws of nature. The intricacies of nature's design and function might be beyond complete understanding, but you don't need to grasp every detail. Nature gives clear signals about whether you're on the right or wrong path. Heed those signals and adjust your course accordingly, and you'll live the best version of yourself while you're here. Once you're gone, what happens afterward is beyond your control or concern. Take the millionaire, for instance, he was dead and still hoped for revival. His body has decomposed, and it doesn't matter now, because he has no awareness of what happens after death."

All you got is when you are alive. Don't just be alive, be awake. Once you're dead, everything else seizes.

The Final Words

I didn't realize it was time for my grandpa's rest again, and the surgery was scheduled for early in the morning. As he slowly spoke about his regrets, I listened intently. He concluded, "I'm done. I feel better now. I've shared everything that was within me to someone; they're out of me for now, not completely though."

I told him, "It's time for you to rest now, Grandpa. You have your surgery scheduled for early in the morning tomorrow. After it's done, you'll be moved out of intensive care, and we can go home after they discharge you in a couple of days."

He gave a gentle smile and replied, "I left my home for the last time already. I don't see myself in it ever again. It's funny how this realization is hitting me now, the place I sat, the home I stayed in, the bed I slept on, the chair I rested in, the people I spoke to, they've all been felt and embraced for the final time, though I didn't realize it then. This hurts too. However, everyone has to leave. Nobody gets to stay forever, and staying forever is not a good experience to chase either. I've told you through the stories already."

I stayed quiet, just listening and allowing his words and emotions to flow.

He continued, "Death is very much unknown. What happens after death is only known by the dead. To know it, you must die. Surprisingly, I felt these emotions when I lost my loved ones. Seeing them die was both depressing and thought-provoking. I couldn't fully comprehend this phenomenon. How can someone who had a physical body a medium for

their senses and expressions just become a non-existent entity, a body that decomposes in no time?

I never understood it completely and perhaps will understand
it sooner."

"To die is to rest; life rests to be alive. The human body is the
greatest and most complex machine on this planet. To run
for so many years without rest makes it deserving of a final
rest when it stops working.

Thus, my body will rest too. It will be gone, buried, or burnt;
it won't exist as you saw it or as I saw it for myself. Its journey will end, and that is the natural course of things."

As my body holds no value, my inner self of being somebody
vanishes too. It must transform into something else, hopeful-
ly, or perhaps it becomes a bygone substance forever.

Remember, kid, if I die, think of it as I'm in need of rest rather than an abrupt exit. I may not come back as this person
or entity, but perhaps my presence will be felt through the
emotions and memories I leave behind, shared with you and
all those who touched my existence, even if only briefly.

I don't fade away from your imagination; the fact that I existed will be a picture in the minds of those left behind, keeping
me alive within them as long as they remember me.

If I'm remembered, that's good. If I'm forgotten, that's better...

Don't hold on to me or dwell on my absence; it doesn't lead
to a better life for you. Whether I'm present or absent should
not disturb your peace. Remember me with a smile, and if

you choose not to think of me, know that I'll still smile, even if only in memory.

Letting me go completely is the best thing, you can do because, let me not regret dying too.

Let death be my liberation than my end. End is when something finishes, to liberate is to move towards another leaving everything behind.

However, I'll still give my best to get through the operation tomorrow. I will strive to come out of it, even if I face death in the process. Death is a feeling experienced by those who live, not by the one who dies. The one who dies does not understand what it is to be dead; only those left behind truly grasp it. I feared death when I was alive, but now that I might be approaching it, I no longer fear it.

I understand that you and our family may not grasp this as easily as I do, but you will eventually move through your grief, forget me, and continue your lives as if I was never there. That's how it should be. It's the healthier way to approach life and death.

You should go home now. Come back early in the morning. If I get a chance, I'll speak with you before I head into the operating room. If not, I've already shared more than enough throughout your life and especially in these past two days.

I was deeply moved, and the grief began to settle in. Still, I tried to focus on his words and honor them first before letting my emotions take over.

"Alright, Grandpa. I'll be here before your operation starts. Everyone else will be here too to speak with you. I'm confident you'll make it through and come back healthy," I replied.

As I was leaving, my grandpa called out gently. I turned back and said, "Yes, Grandpa?"

"Take care of yourself," he said. "I had good memories with you. Don't mourn over my lifeless body when I'm gone. Instead, look at me with pride, knowing I lived my life fully. Though I had regrets, my life is complete. Whether it was a success or a failure, I experienced it all. Everyone will eventually leave, and now it's my turn. If there is a place where the dead gather, I'll meet my parents, brother, and friends. I'll wait for all of you. Don't come to me too soon. Keep me waiting as long as you can. Goodbye."

I smiled gently, pushing through the overwhelming grief, and made my way back home. The surgery was scheduled for nine the next morning, and sleep was elusive. My mind couldn't escape the haunting thought of my grandpa's death. His words and our conversation lingered, making me fear the worst. Yet, a sliver of hope kept me believing that a miracle might happen and he would come through safely.

The next morning, I woke before sunrise and rushed to the hospital. My grandmother and the rest of the family were already there, speaking to my grandfather, offering words of reassurance that he would come out safe. I carried his medical reports, an extra set of clothes for him to change into after discharge, and his shoes, which weren't permitted in the operating theater.

The doctors informed us that the operation would take twenty to thirty minutes. Grandpa was wheeled into the operating room on a stretcher. As we watched him go, he gave us a thumb-up gesture, but with a downward tilt, as if to subtly signal that we shouldn't hold out too much hope for his return.

My family and I waited outside the operating room; our anxiety palpable. The doctors went inside, and the doors closed behind them. I kept glancing at my watch, each tick feeling like an eternity, hoping for the moment when a doctor would emerge to announce that the operation had been a success.

The twenty-minute surgery stretched into thirty, forty, then fifty minutes without any word from the doctors. Finally, after an hour and six minutes, the surgeon emerged from the operating room. He asked us to follow him to his office. We rushed to his cabin, our hearts pounding, eager for any news about my grandfather's condition.

The surgeon, his voice heavy with sadness, delivered the grim news: "We encountered an unforeseen perforation inside his body, making stent placement impossible. He suffered a heart attack during the surgery, was revived, but then experienced another heart attack. He's now on a ventilator, and I fear he may not survive."

We rushed to see my grandfather. The perforation had caused air leakage, known as emphysema, and his condition was so dire that he was barely recognizable. Unsure if he could even hear us, I couldn't bear to see him in such a state and stepped out of the room, overwhelmed by the sight.

A few minutes later, another doctor emerged with my grandfather's heartbeat report and delivered the final verdict: his heart had stopped, and he had taken his last breath.

The experiences, words, laughter, and grief we shared together had become memories, frozen in time. I found myself unable to cry; my mind, in an effort to cope, had adjusted to the reality of his absence, struggling to grasp the enormity of his departure.

His medical reports, clothing, and shoes were left behind at the hospital while his body was taken away for the rituals. I had never felt this way before; his absence was profoundly real, yet his presence remained as if he had never truly departed. His words were etched into me, especially from the two days before he left. His life experiences and regrets, shared so openly, made me reflect deeply. I thought that if I followed his advice wisely, avoiding the regrets he had felt and striving to improve my own life, perhaps he would find some measure of happiness. You could do the same for him and yourself. That concludes my grandpa's **Twelve Regrets from the Deathbed.**